This Art Nude Model Does Not Exist

I0512327

By Jansen Tableau

All of the images in this book are artistic nude photographs, but there was no model, no camera, no photo shoot. We typed some text in a box, and then then the images happened. The images in this book aren't perfect, and they have been curated from a massive set, generated over a very short time. Some are badly flawed, while some are almost flawless. It takes less than a minute to generate a grid of twelve, although they need upscaling (another AI process) and then they often need to have their faces fixed. StableDiffusion is the generator we used because none of the others would even let us (obviously none of this material is safe for work)

These are what we can make now, today - two years ago this was beyond what we could imagine. Now, think about what five more years will bring?

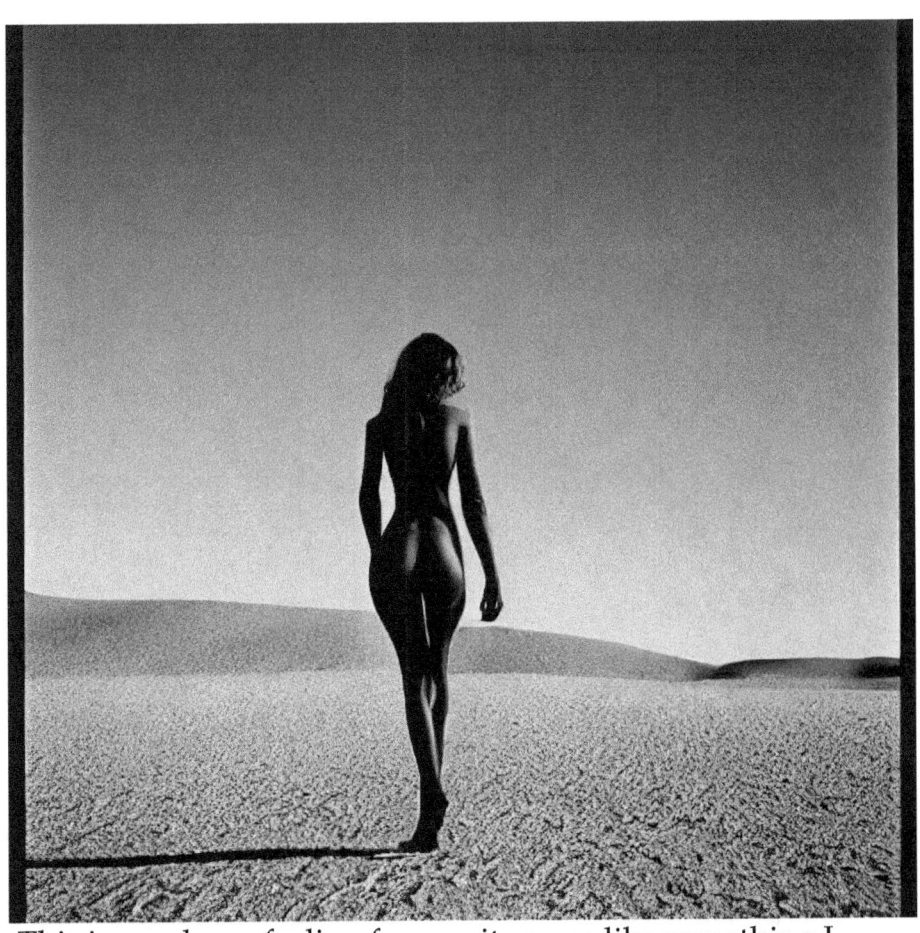

This image has a feeling for me, it seems like something I would admire in a gallery.

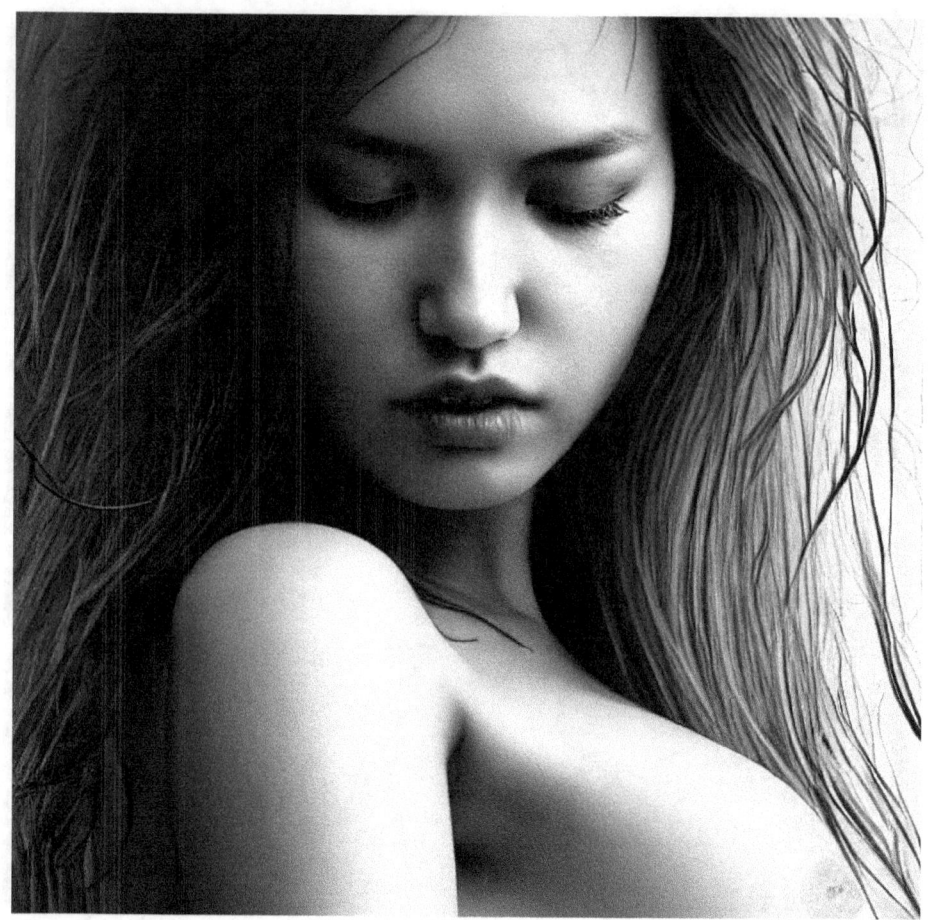

Some of the images feel too slick, too produced, to me. I admire them technically, but I prefer a more organic, messy feel.

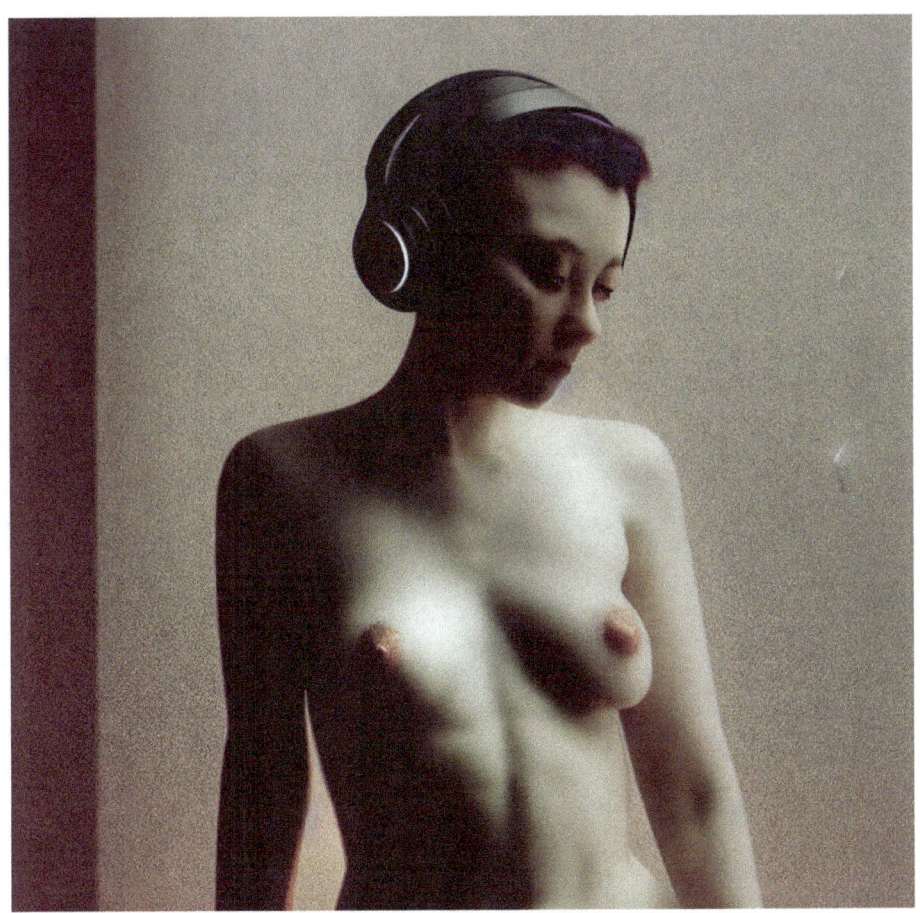

This image has something, I like it a lot - the colours, the tone of it.

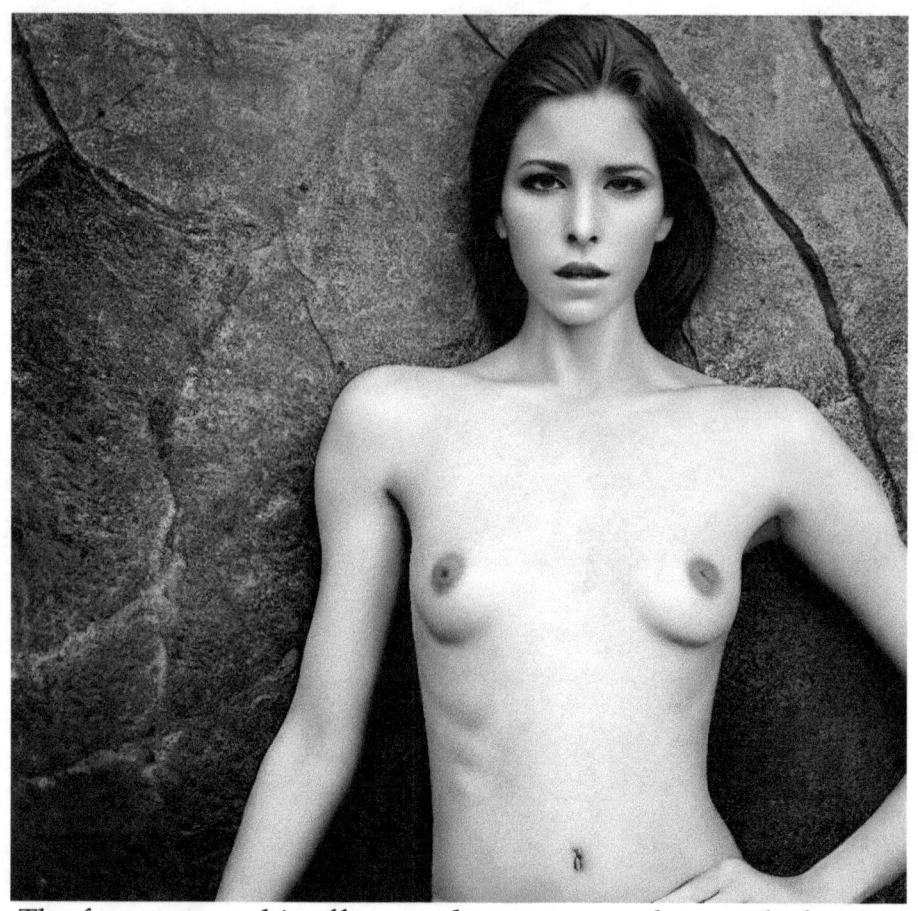
The face seems a bit off to me, but not enough to exclude it, and I like the composition.

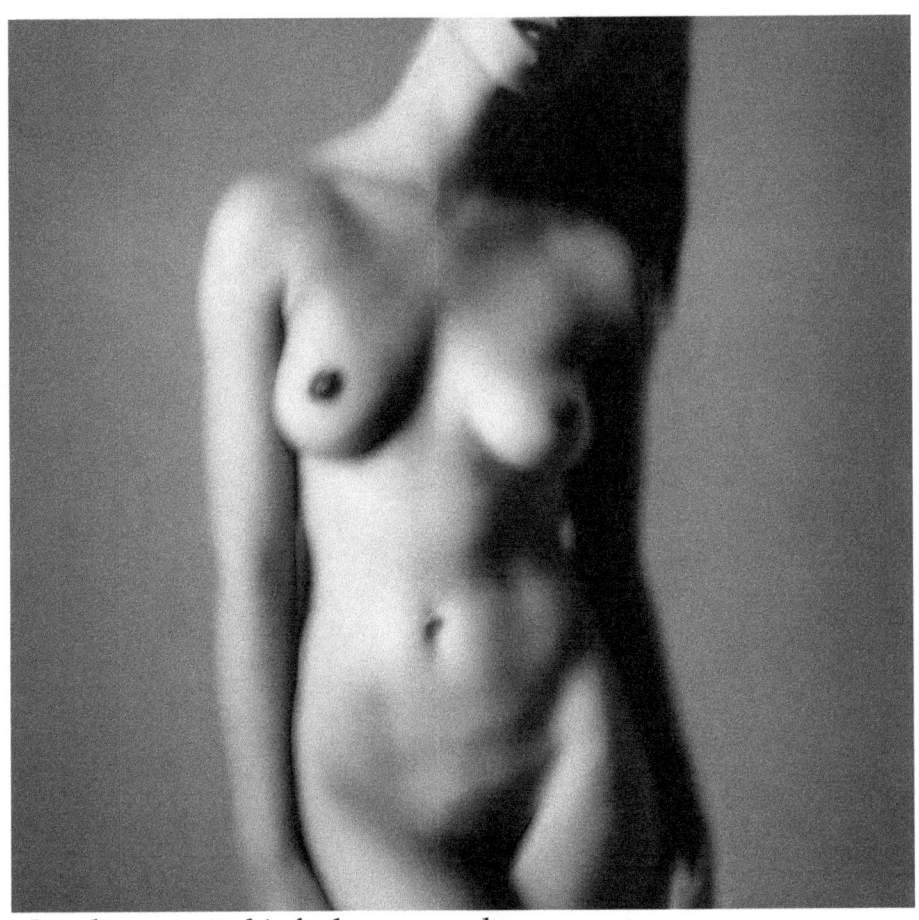
Good tones, and it feels very real to me

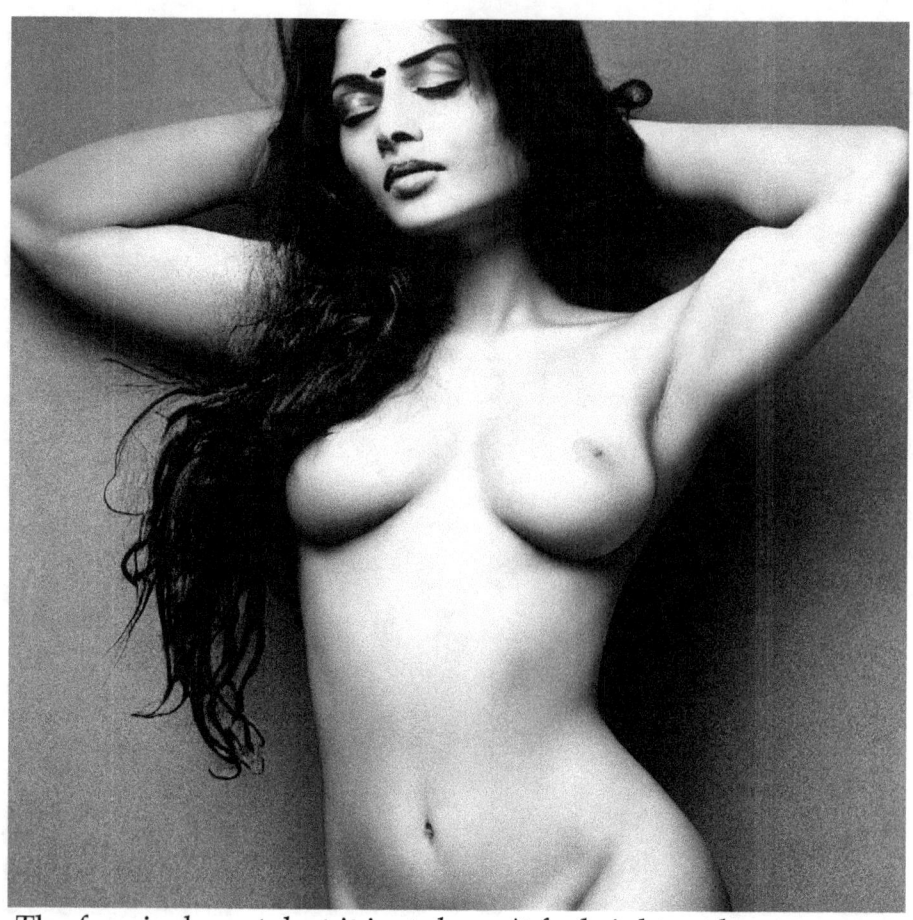

The face is decent, but it just doesn't feel right, at least to my eyes

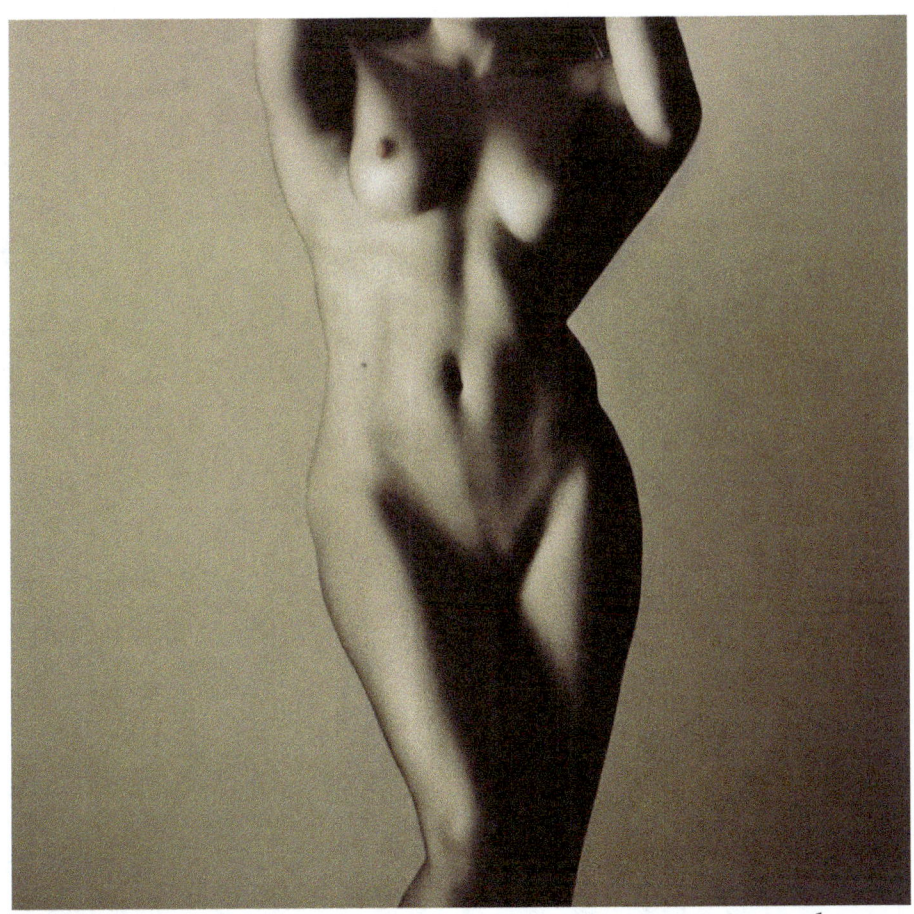

This was the first image that I was certain was going to be included

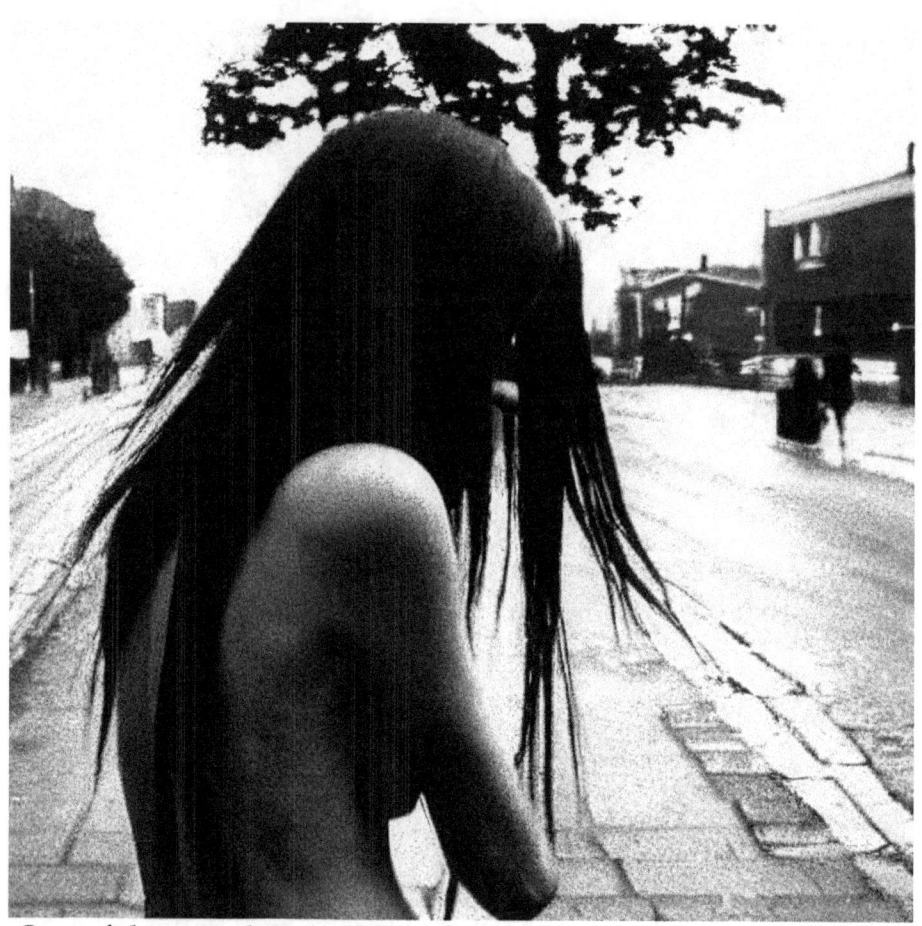

One of the weird ones. I think in a gallery it would do well, as would many of the weird ones

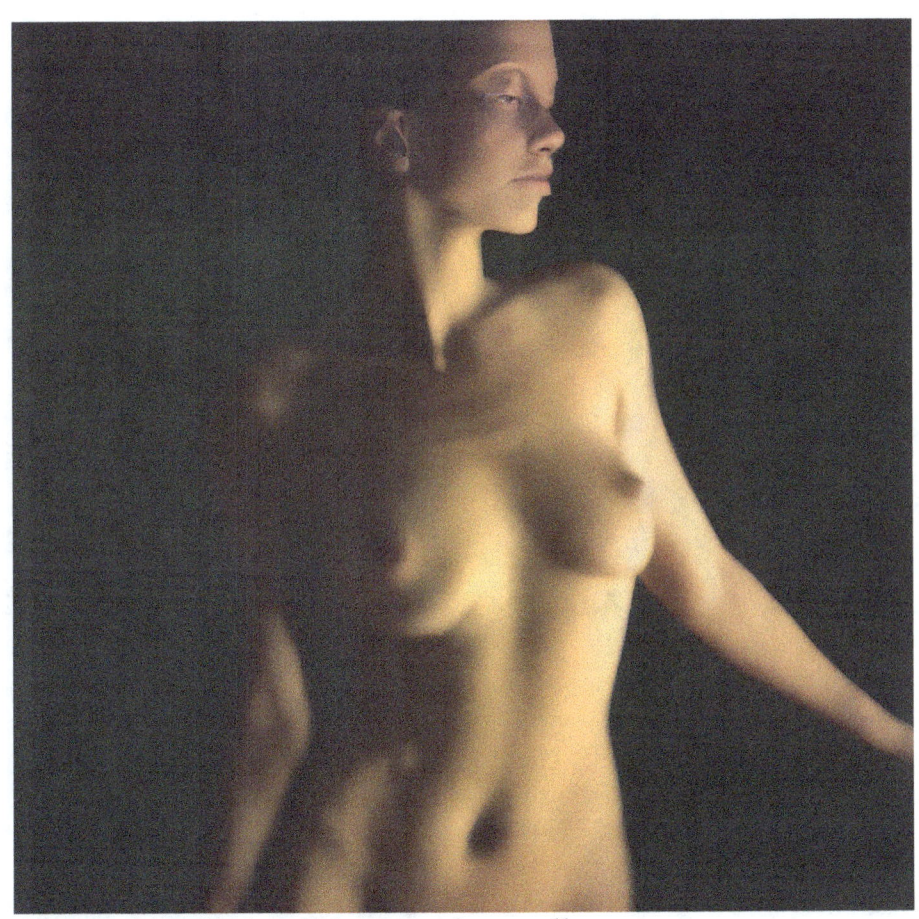
The face is a little off, but good overall

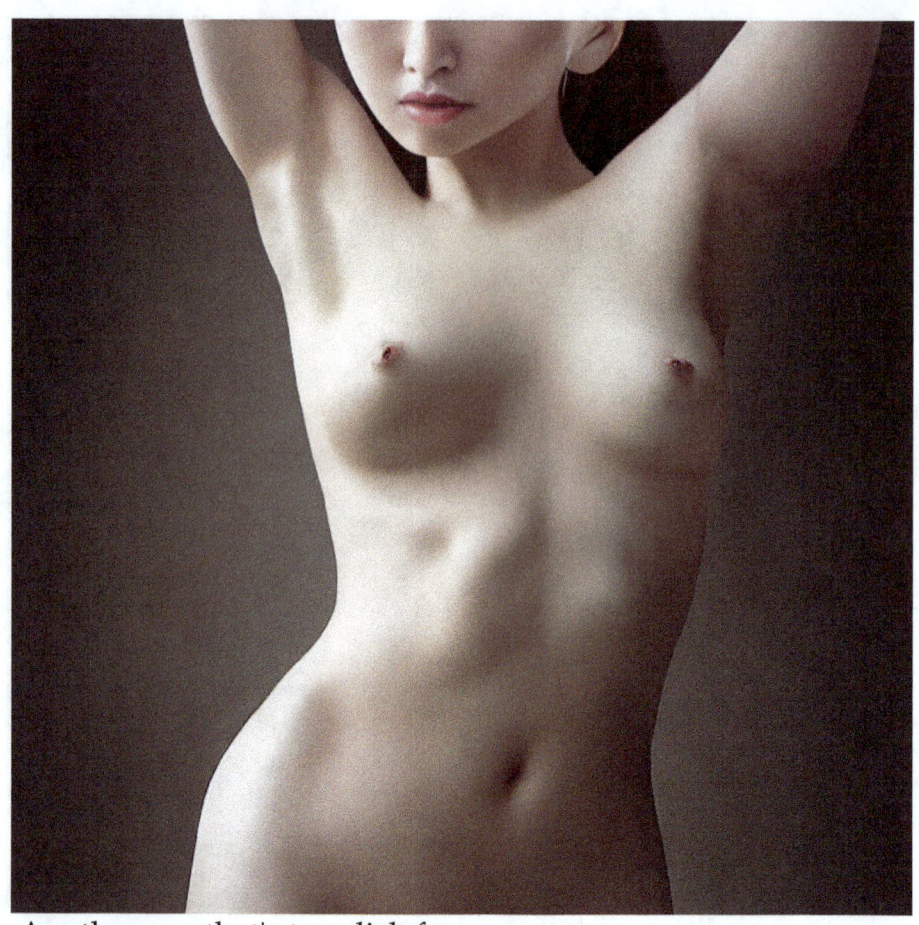
Another one that's too slick for my taste

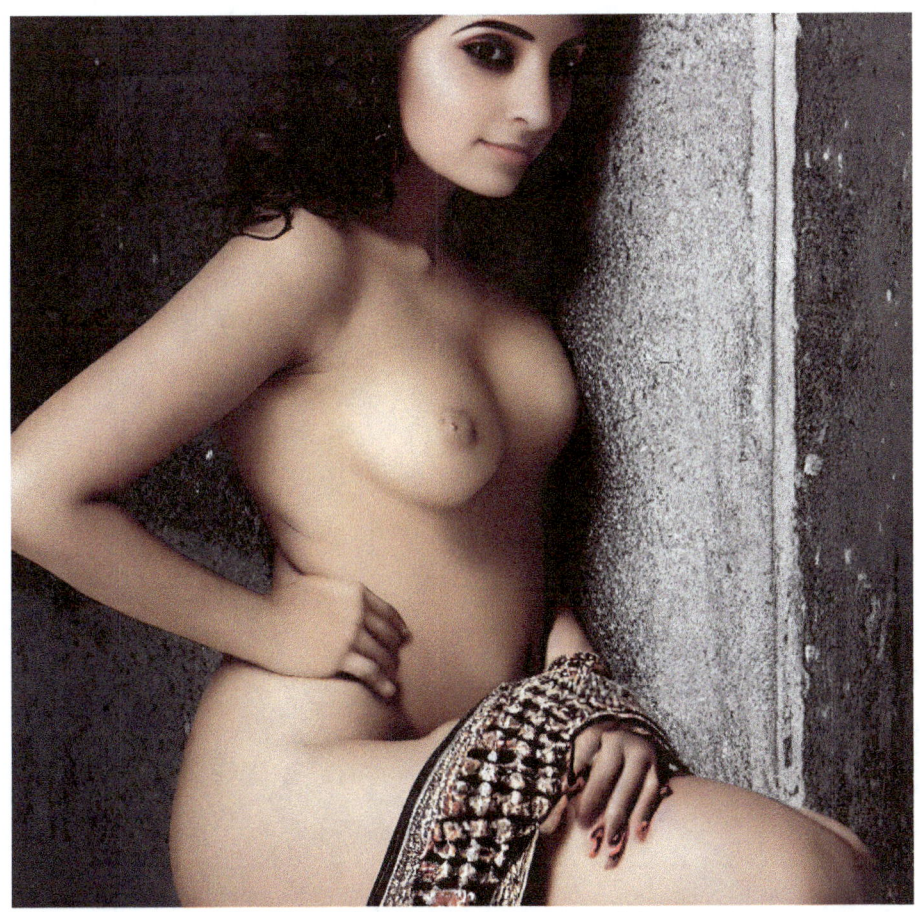
The eyes are off, other than that it's a great image

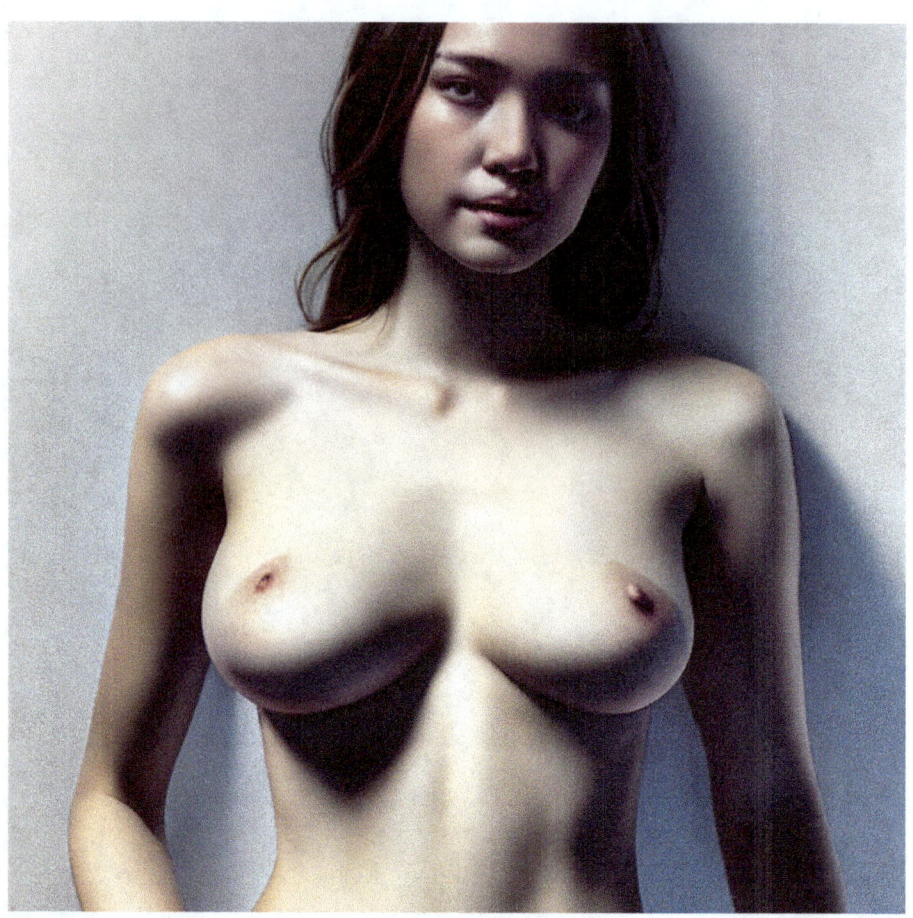
Another of the slick ones, but I like the face

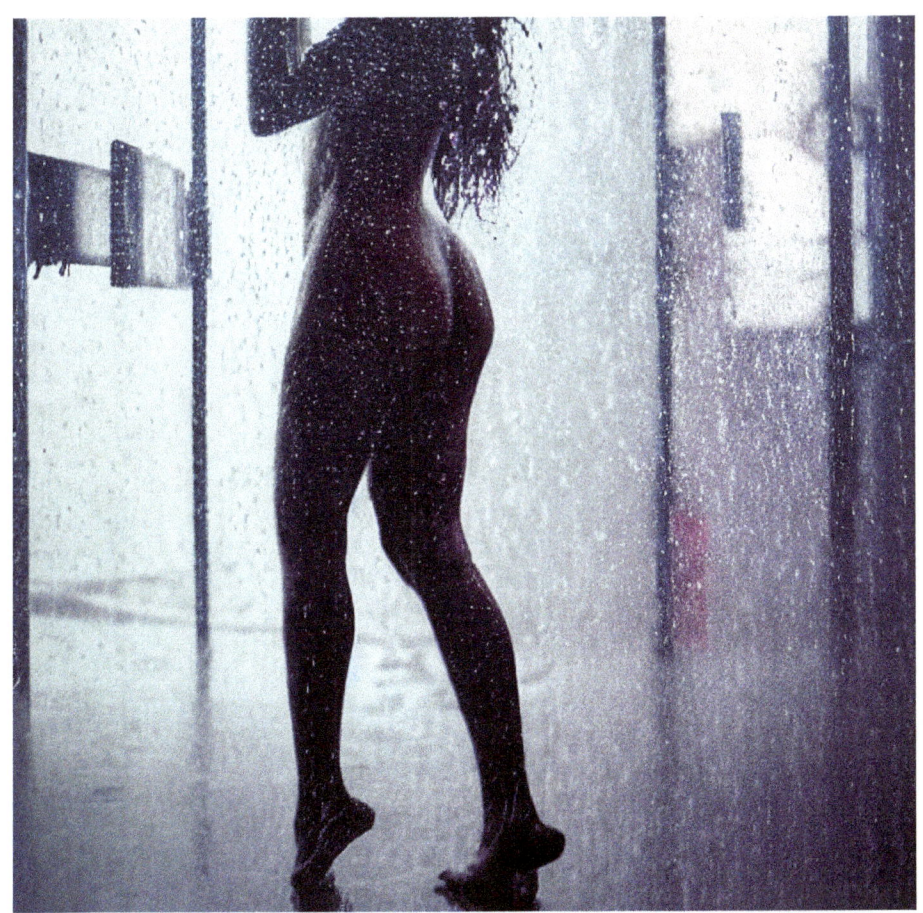
Has an interesting quality to it.

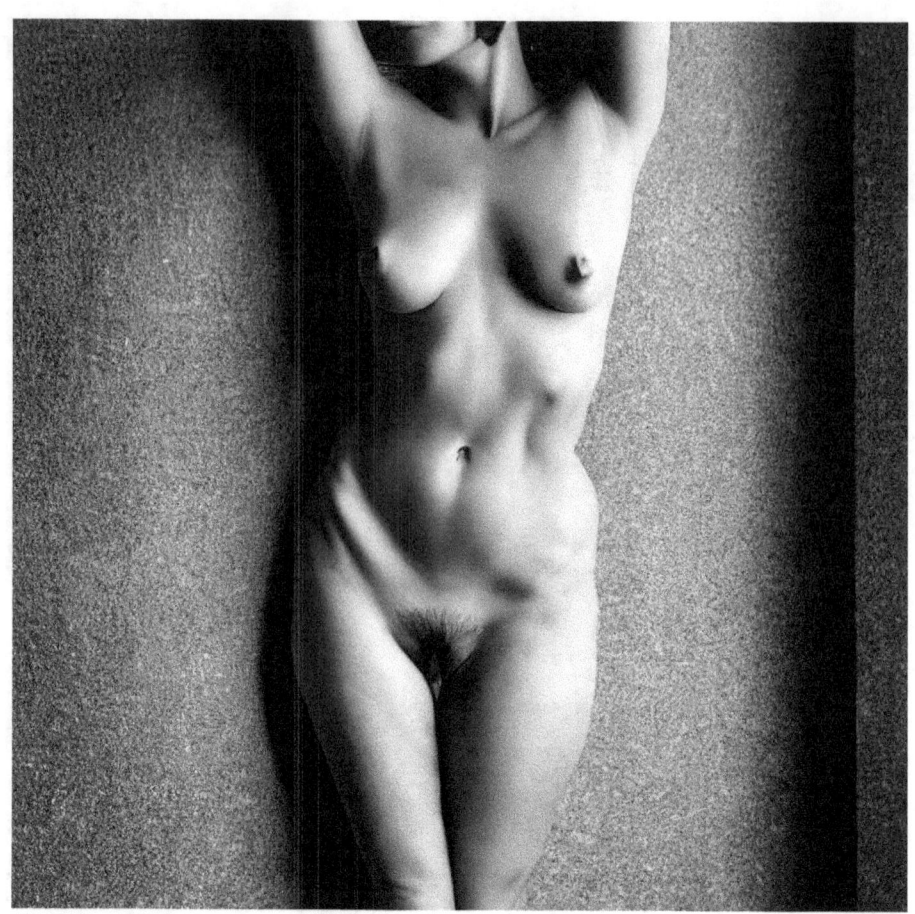
Tones, and it manages to look quite real

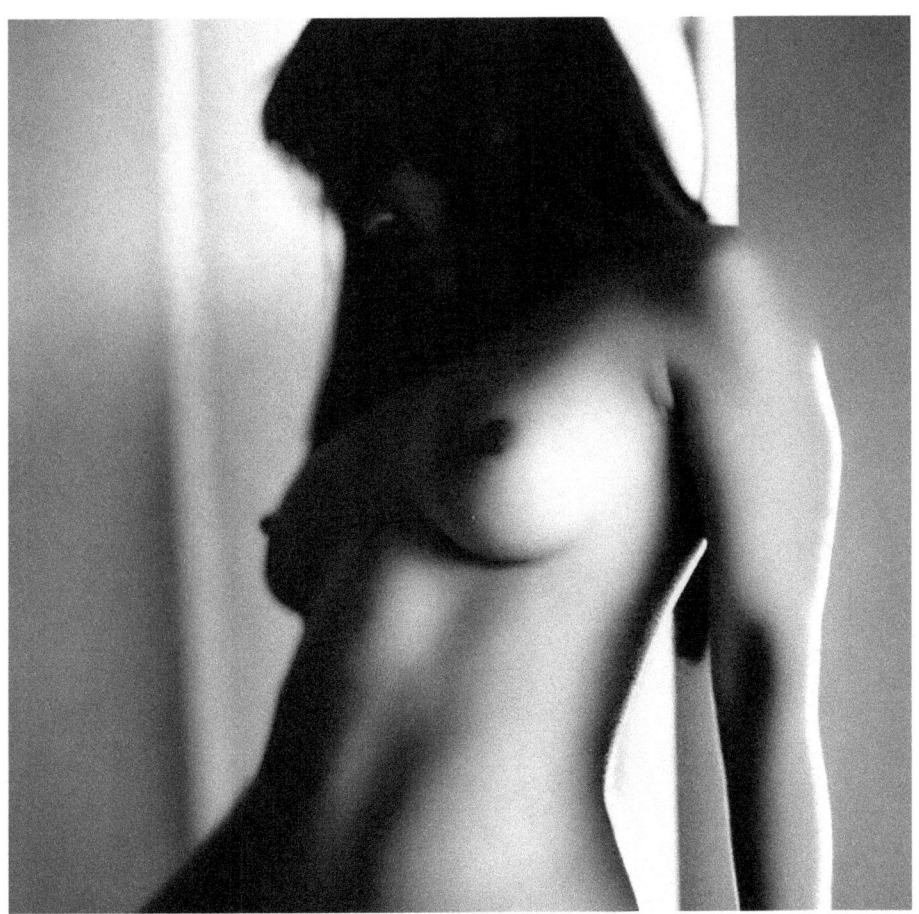

Another one with good tones. The face being shadowed makes it easier

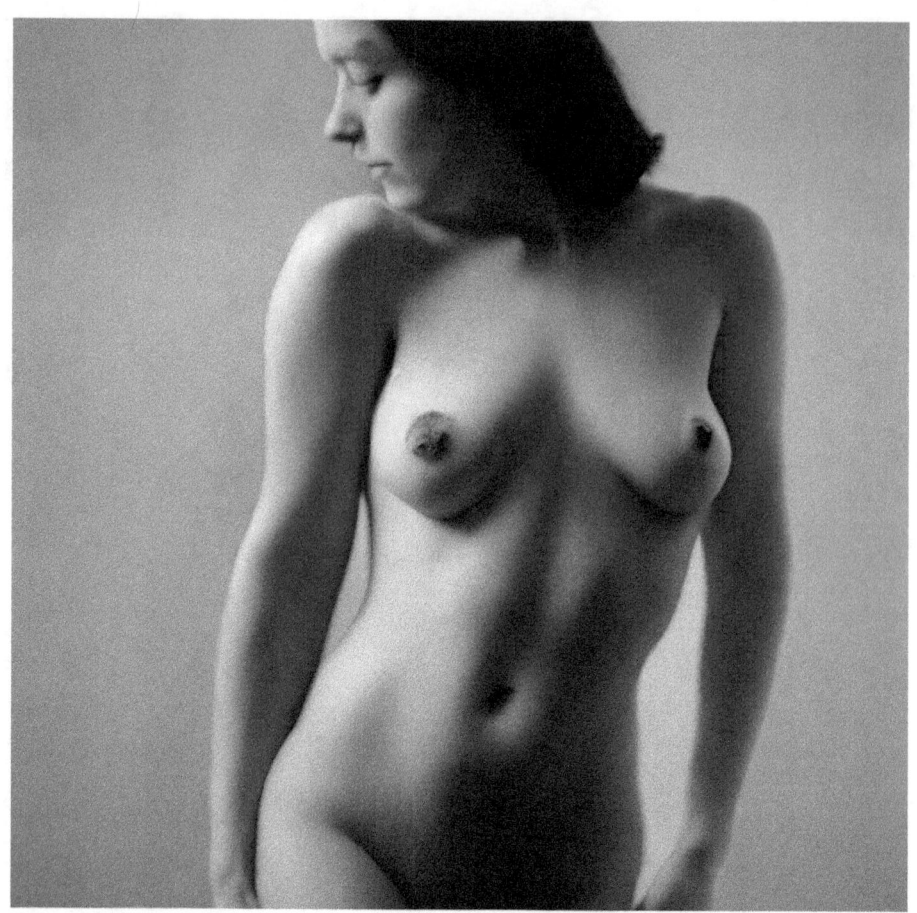

The nipples didn't quite turn out, but otherwise this one would fool me into thinking it was a real photo

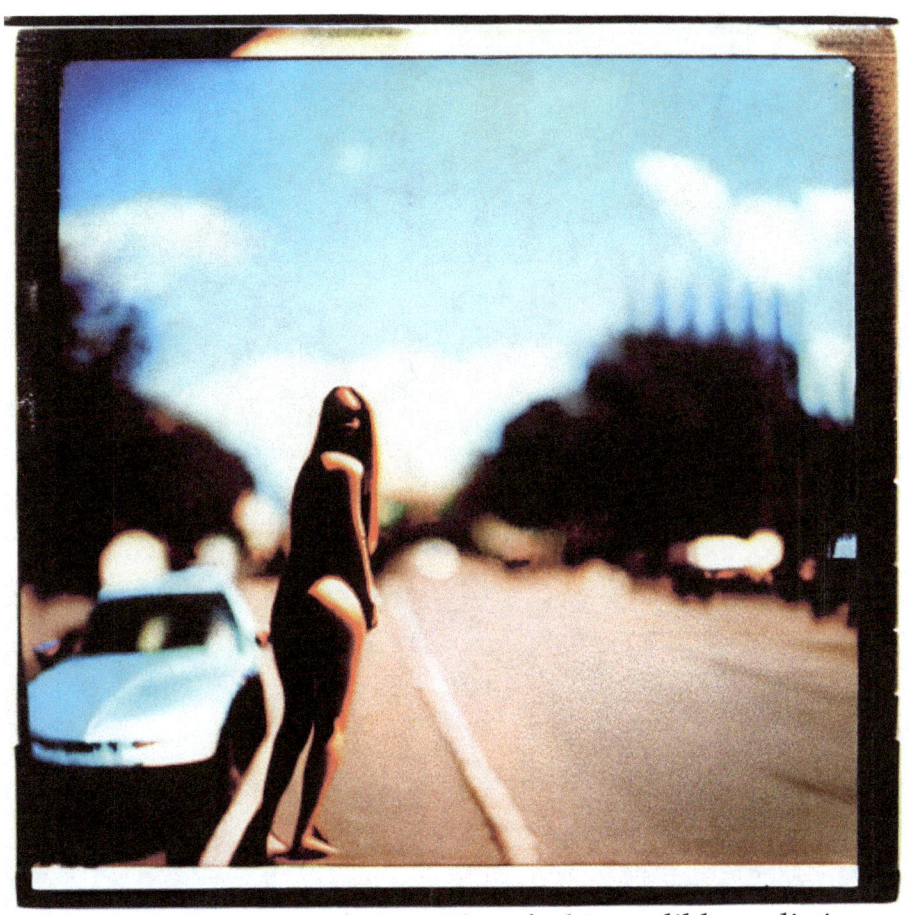

The polaroids are interesting. They feel incredibly realistic and valid to me

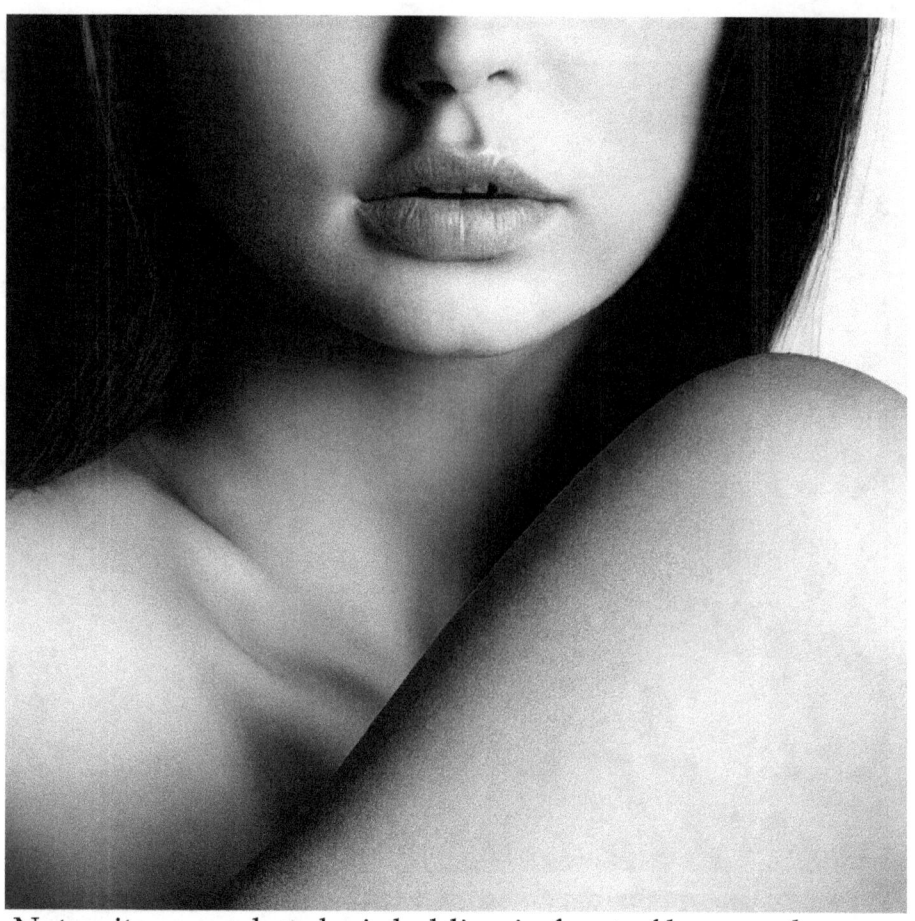
Not quite sure what she is holding in front of her, maybe an arm, maybe an appendage humanity has not yet developed

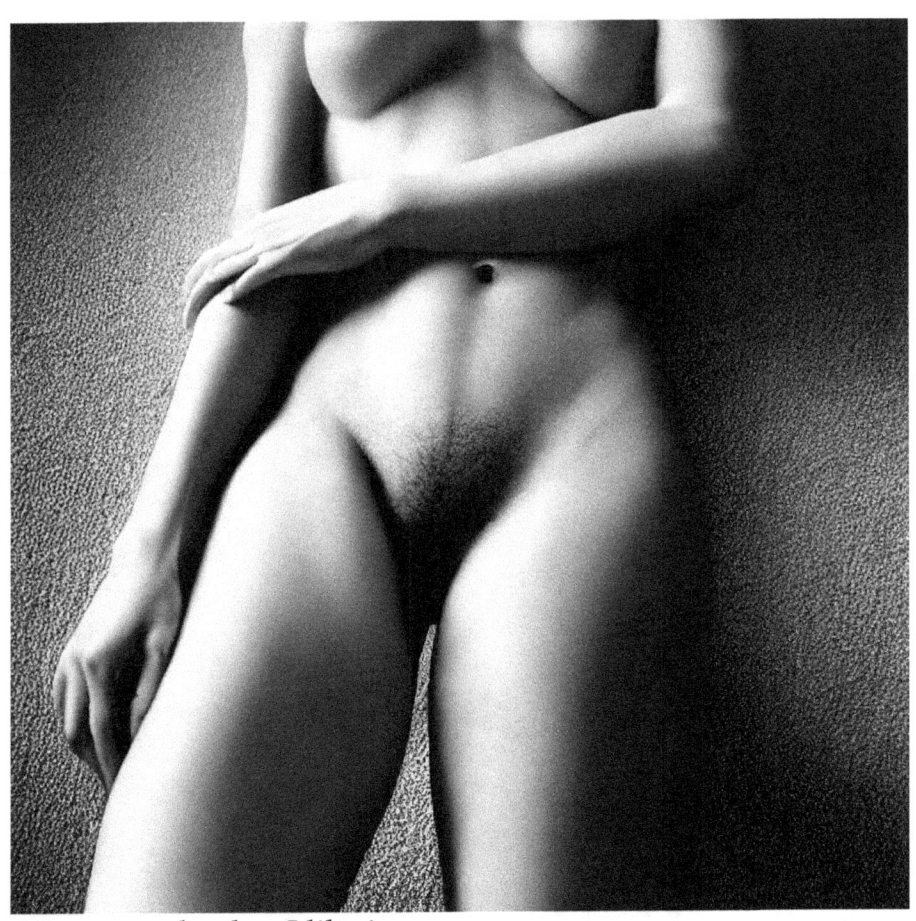
Not sure why, but I like it

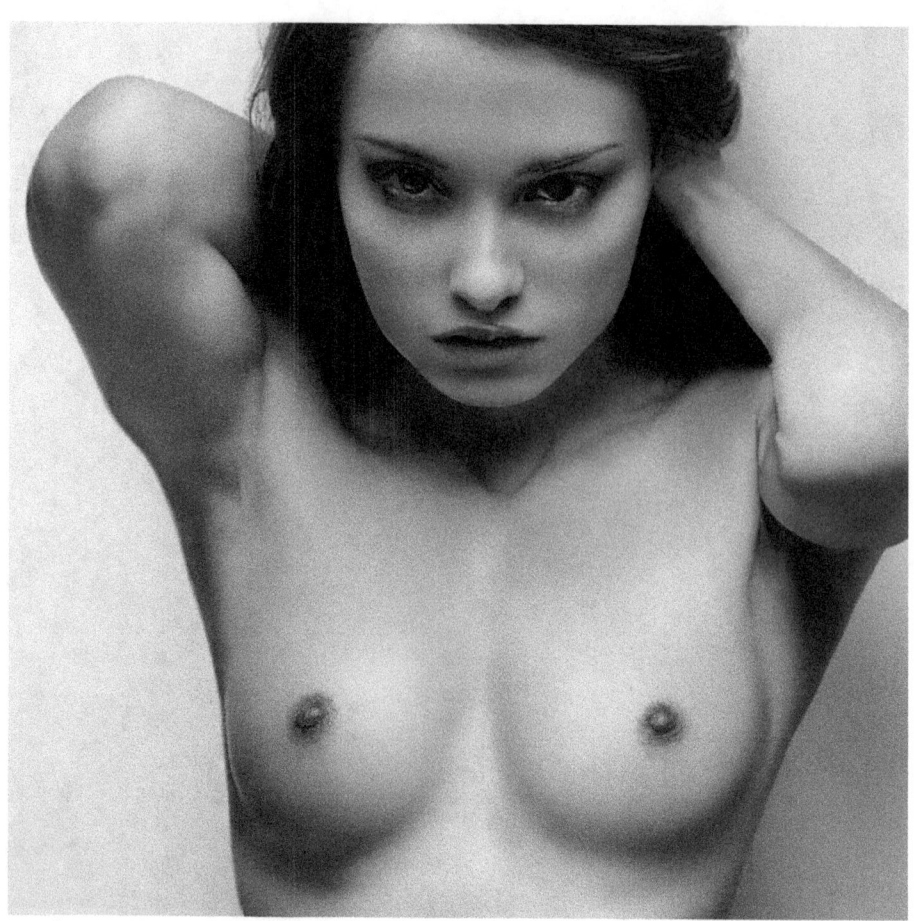
A fierce facial expression

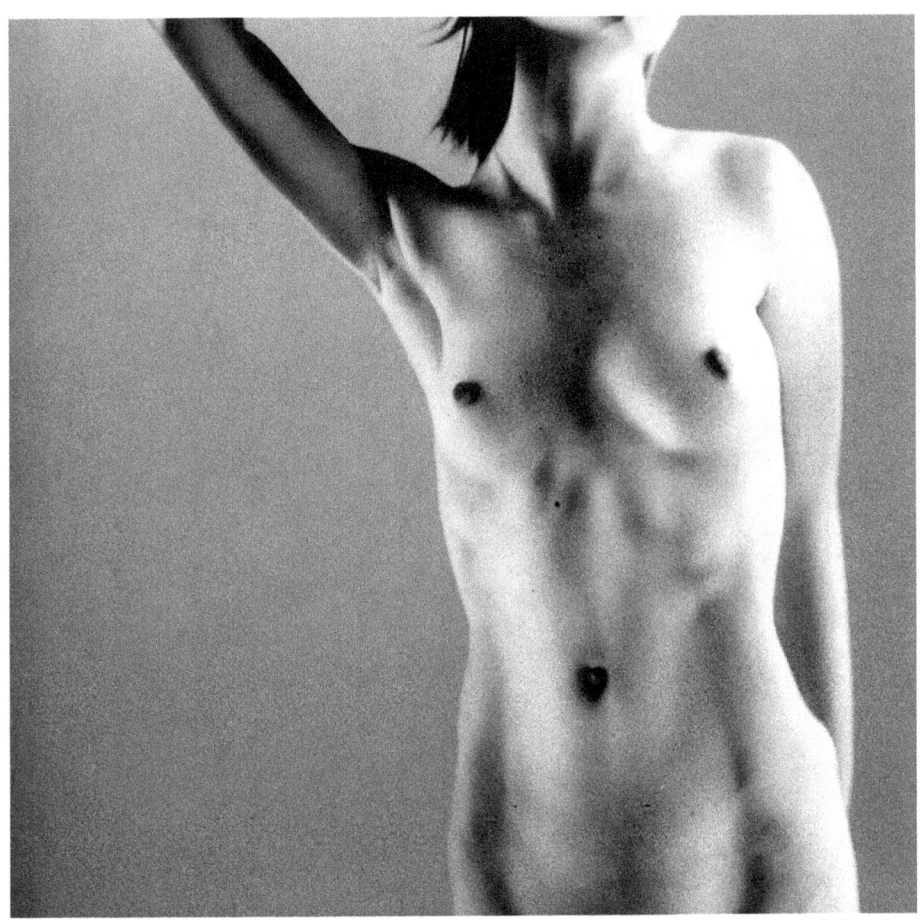

A long, lean body - I think that this one would fool me if I didn't know it was an AI gen

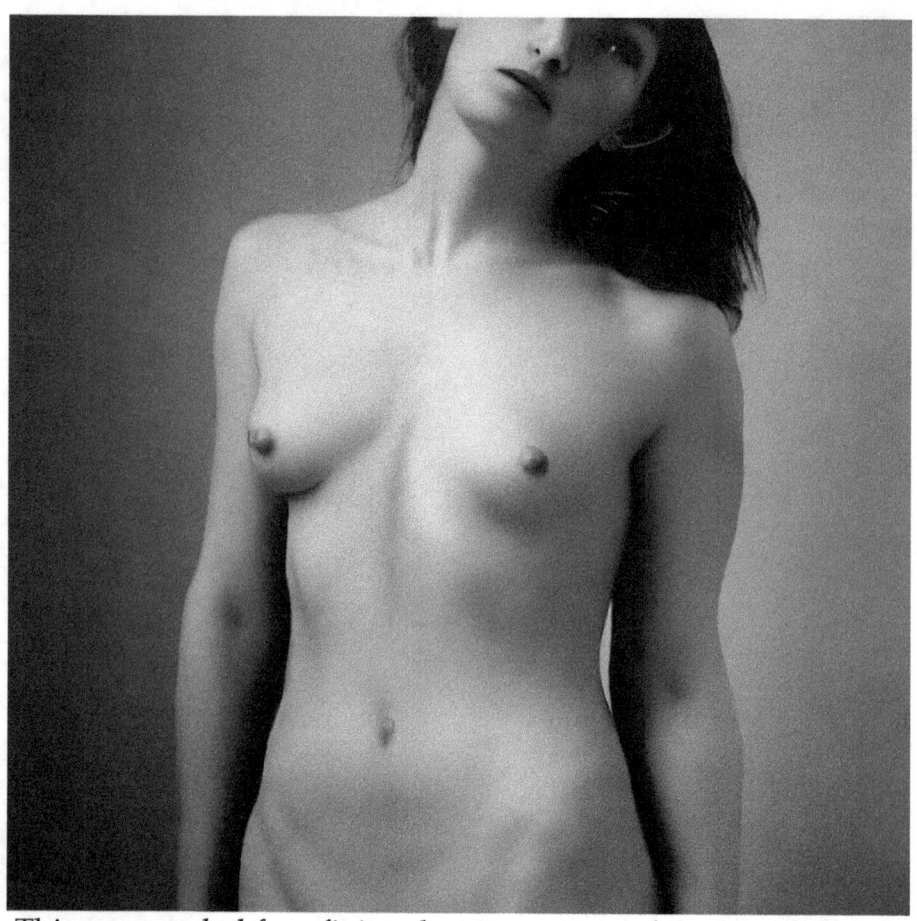
This one needed face fixing, but it was one of the best face fixes I've seen

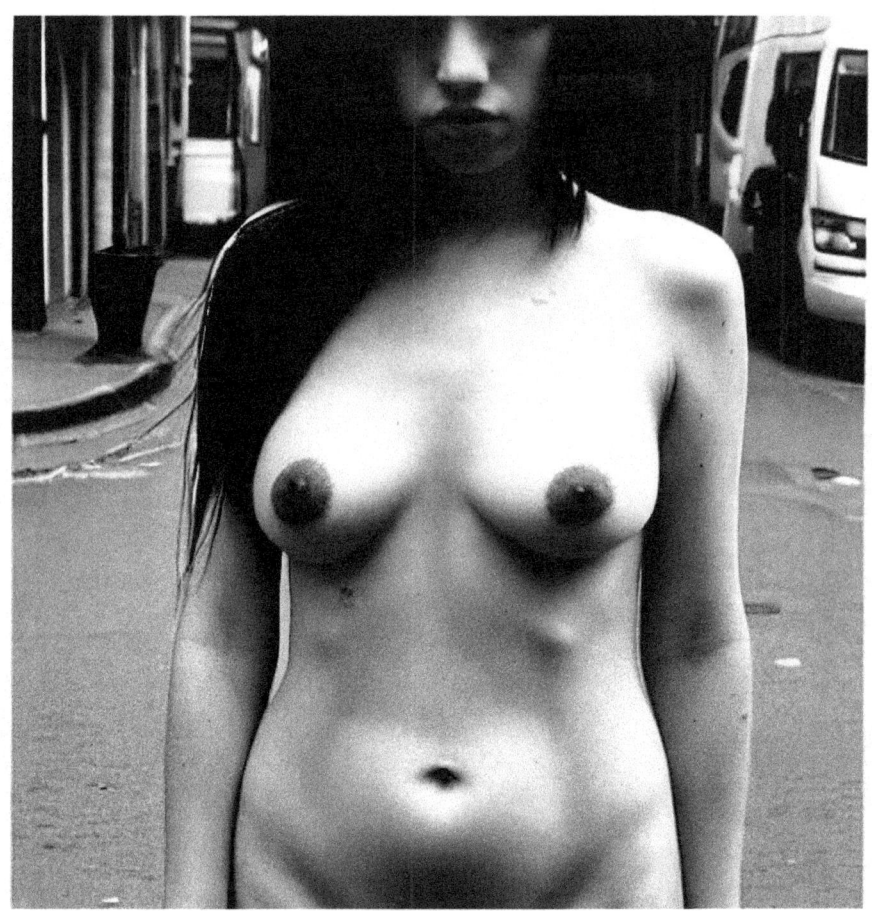

This is the kind of creepy art nude that gets positive press, not sure if anyone really likes it though

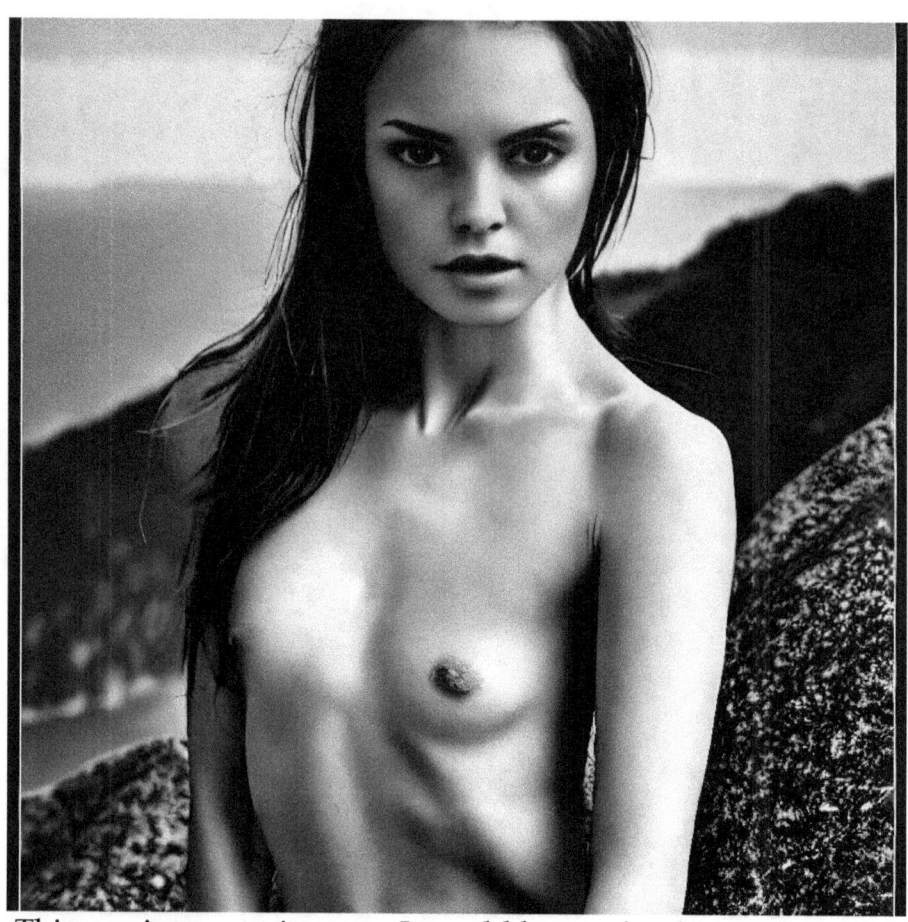

This one is a great image... I would be prod to have taken it had I done so

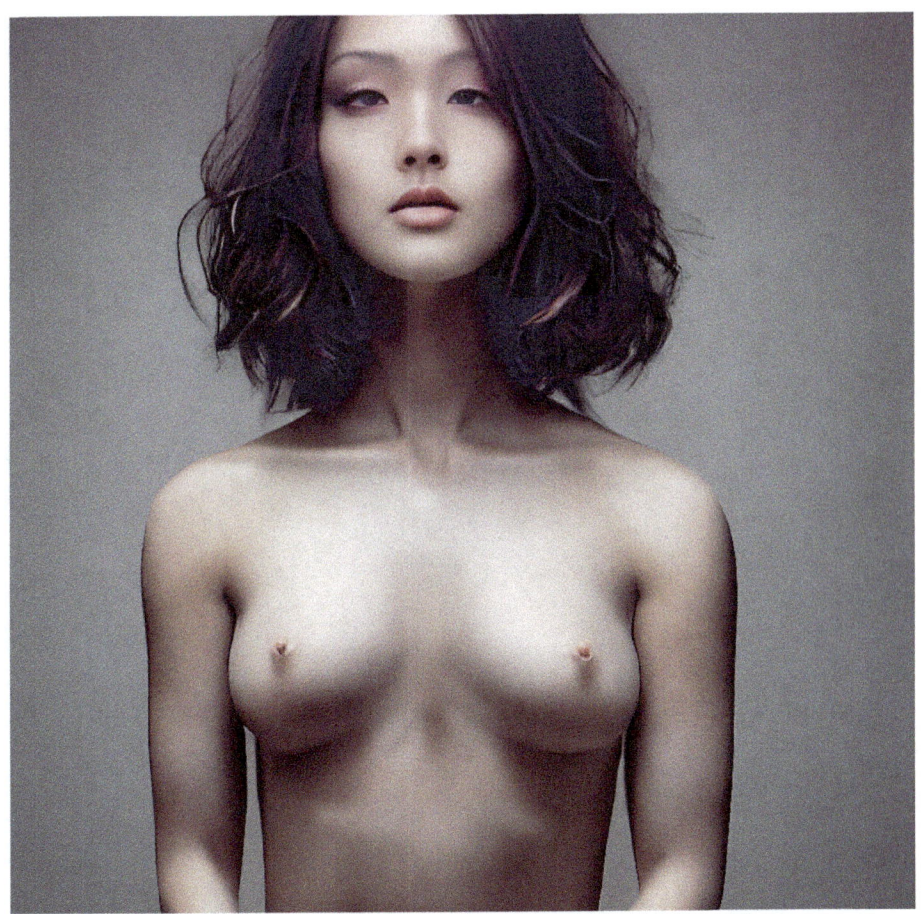

One of the slick ones. Also, the face fixing didn't quite work on the eyes

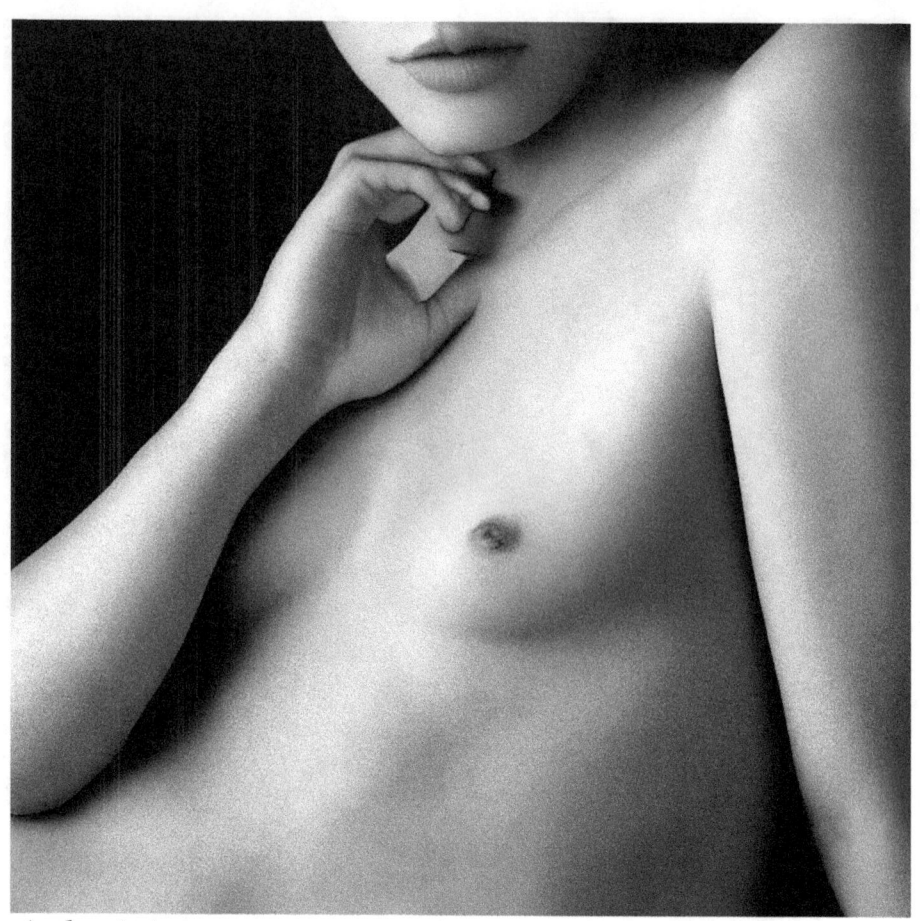

A classic image

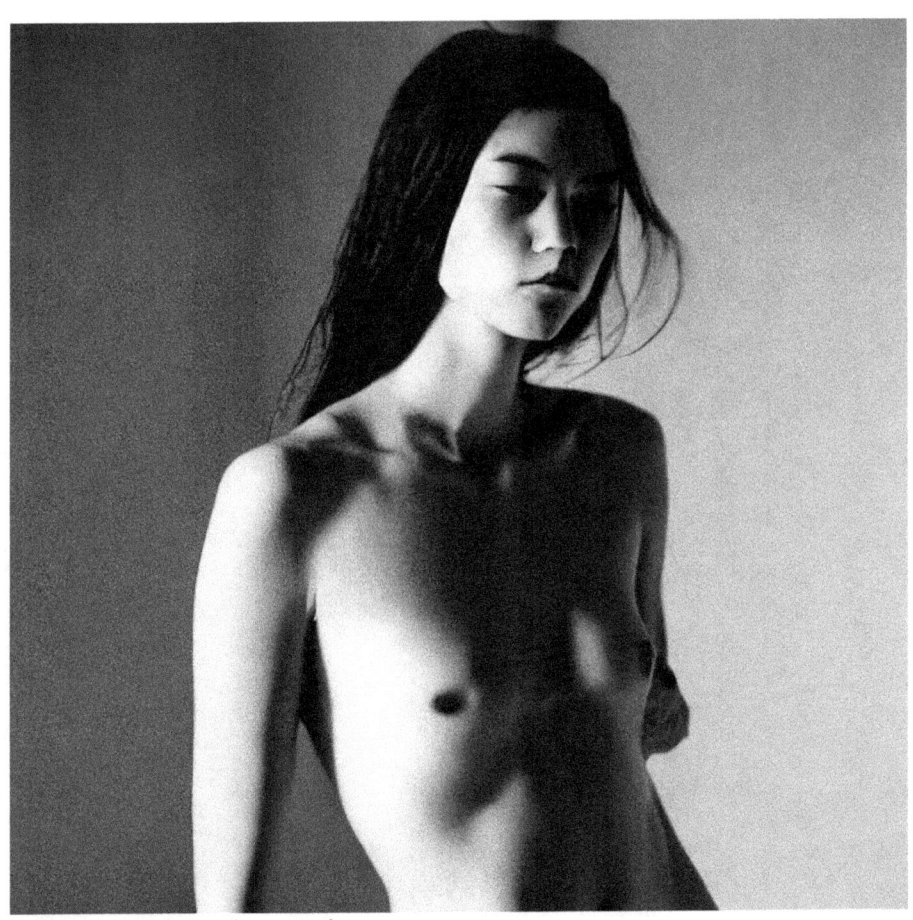
Not one of the better faces

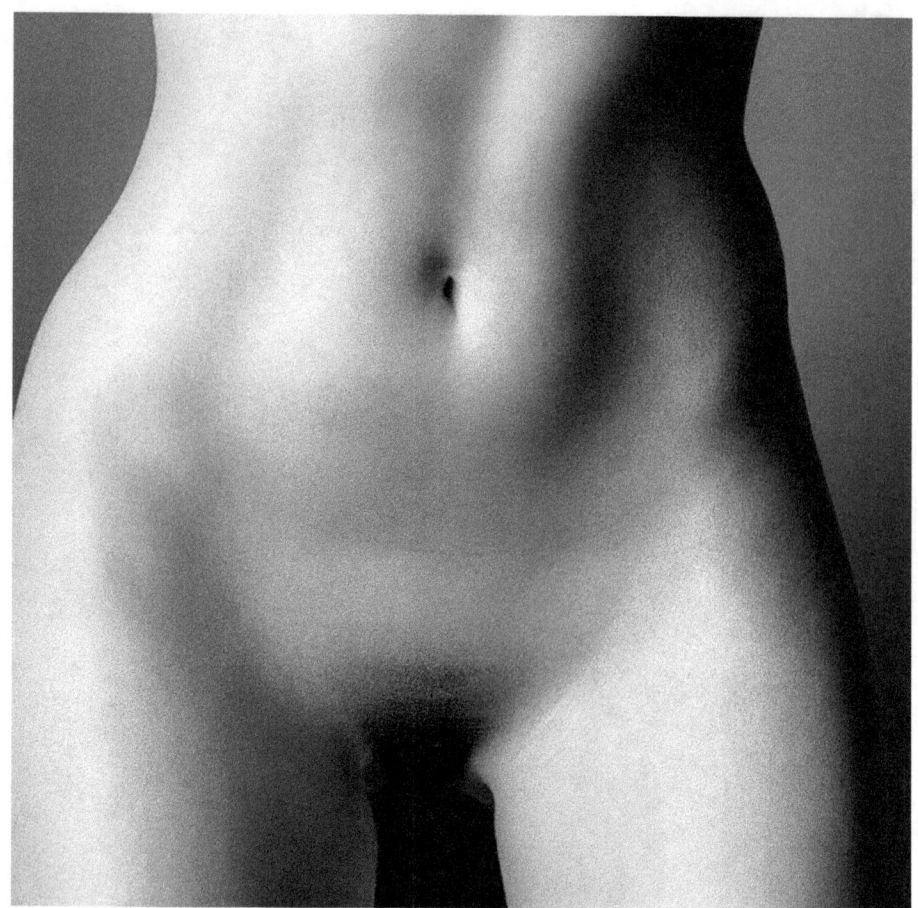
A well done image, even if it would produce some negative comments in a gallery show

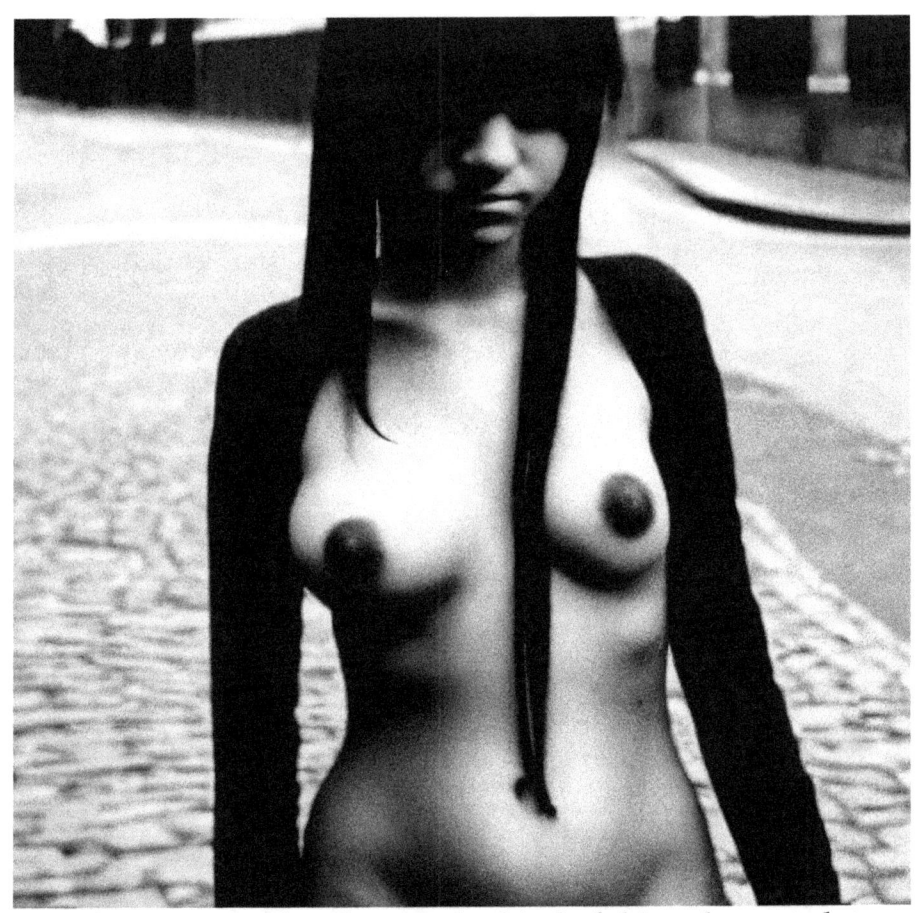

Another creep goth polaroid, the kind of thing that gets lots of hipster cred

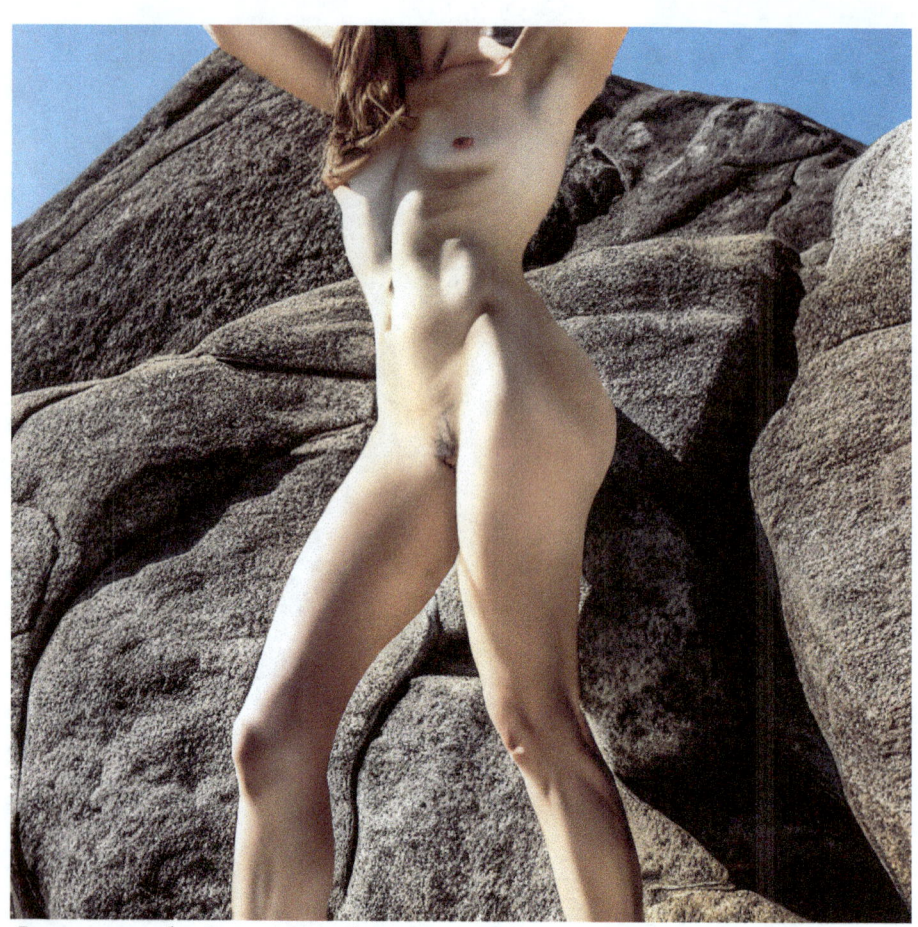
Just a good picture, nothing special

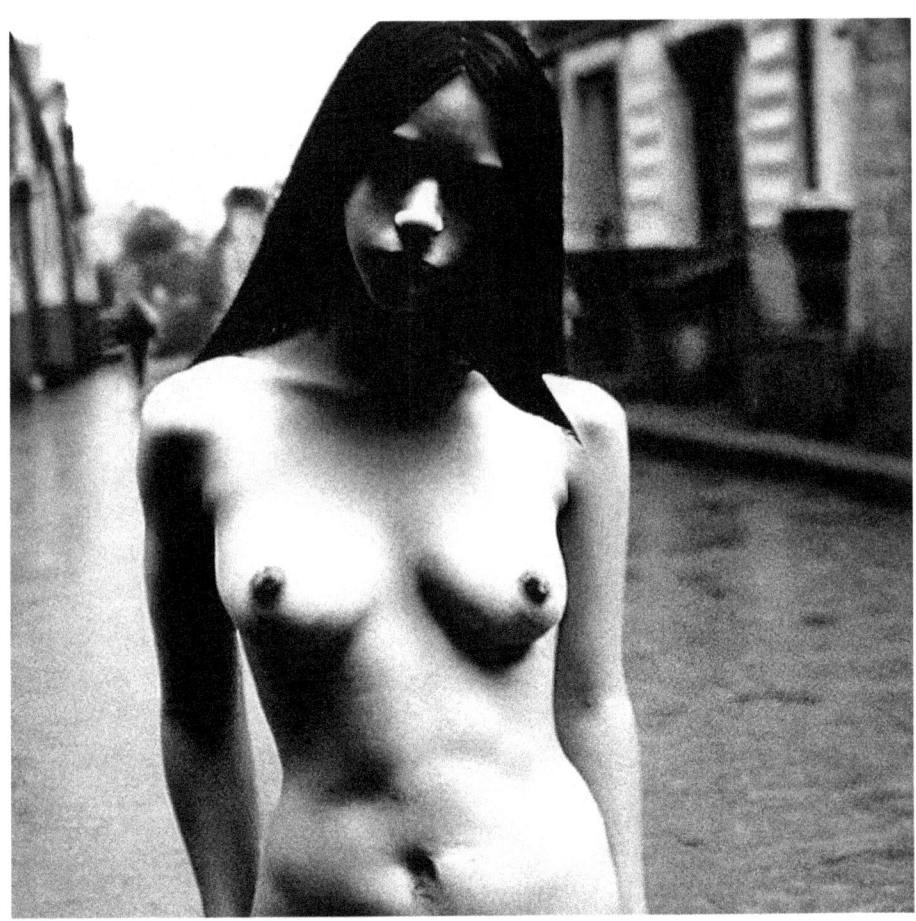
This one is super creepy

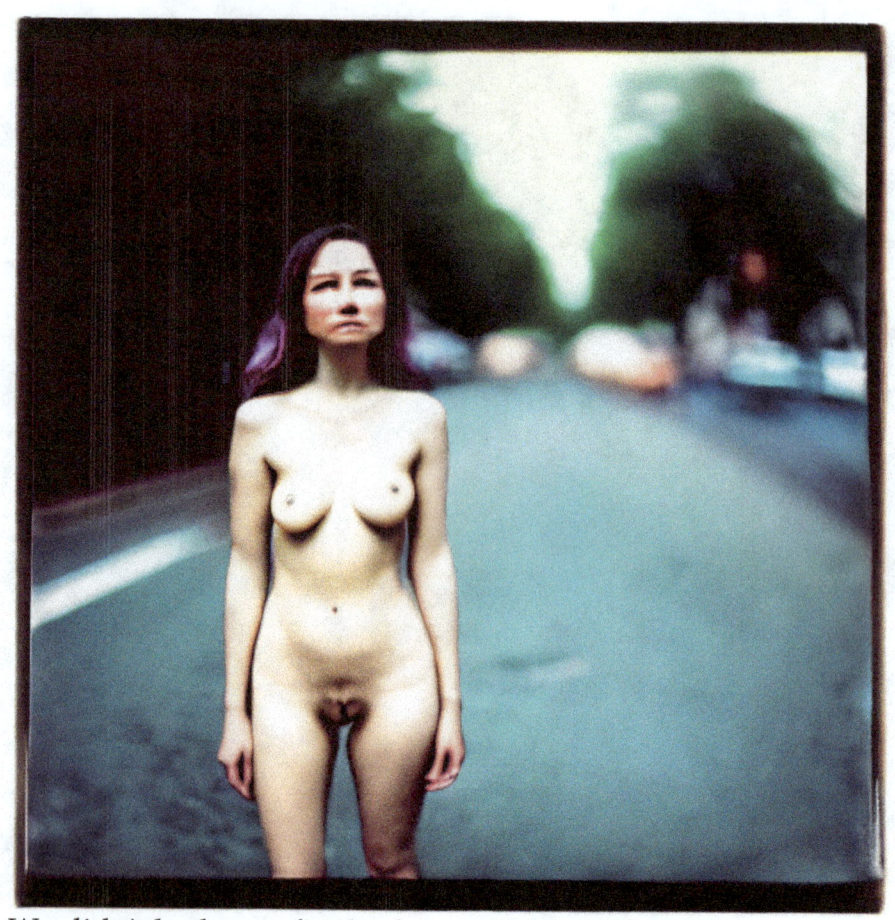
We didn't bother to fix the face on this one, because it somehow matches the quality of the image

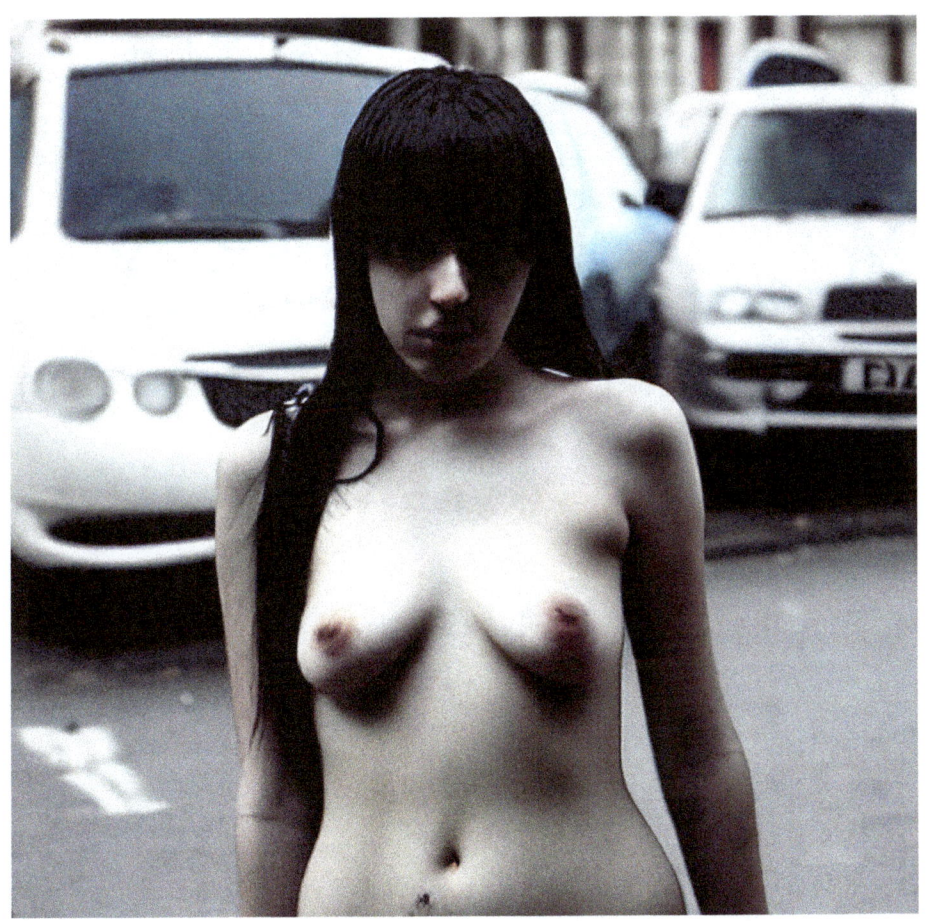
Creepy

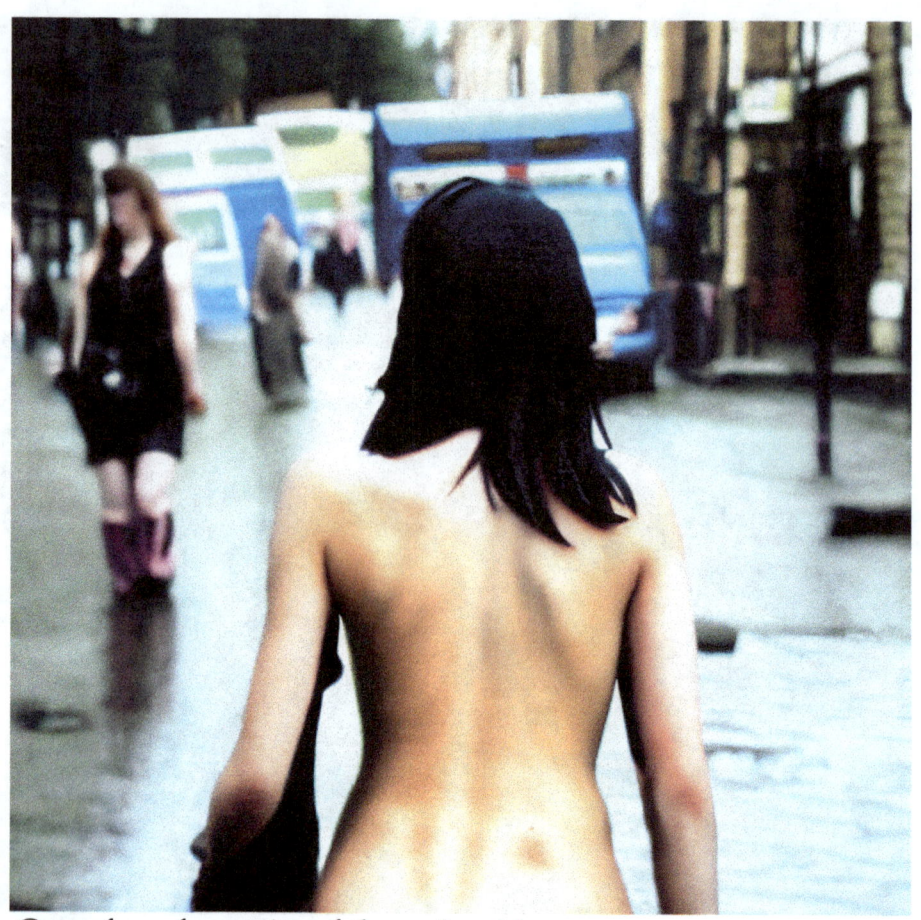
One of my favourite of the polaroid set

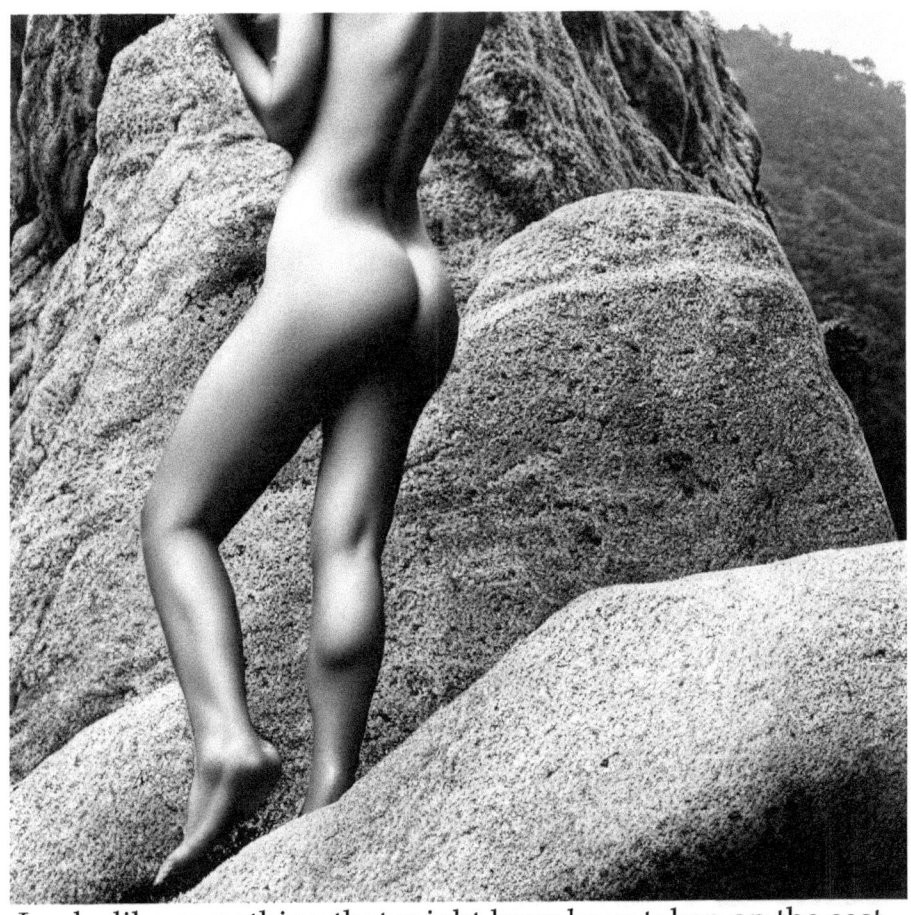
Looks like something that might have been taken on the east coast

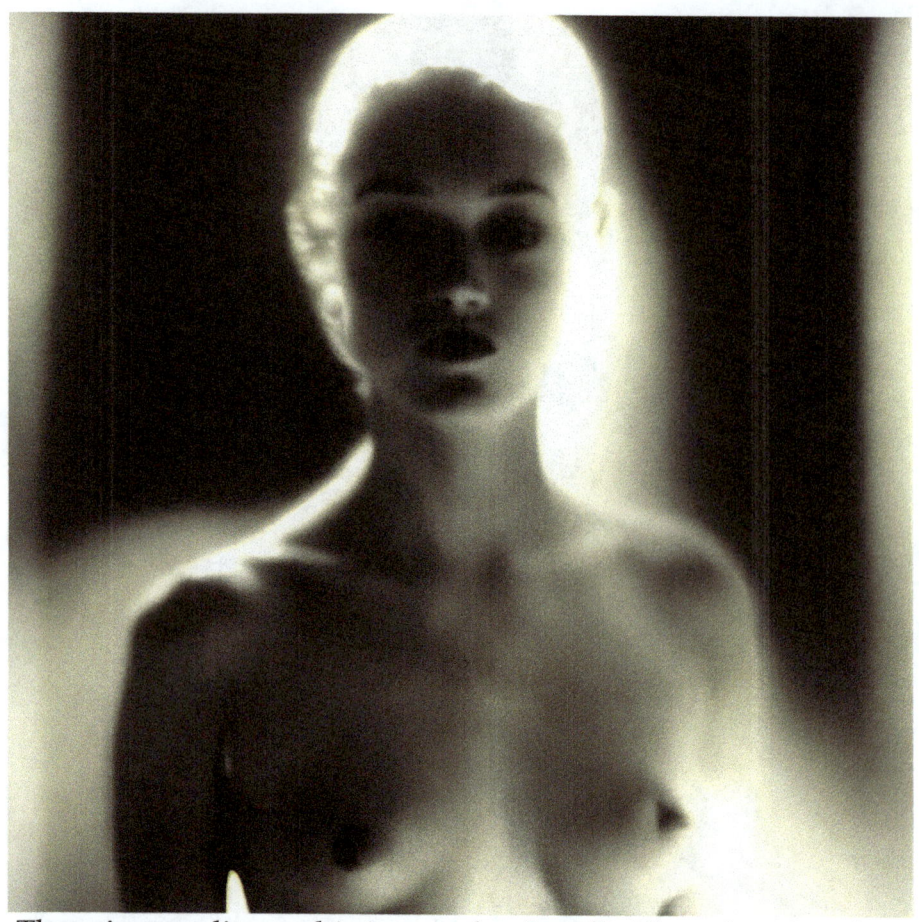

There is a quality to this image that I really like - the sort of spectral light thing

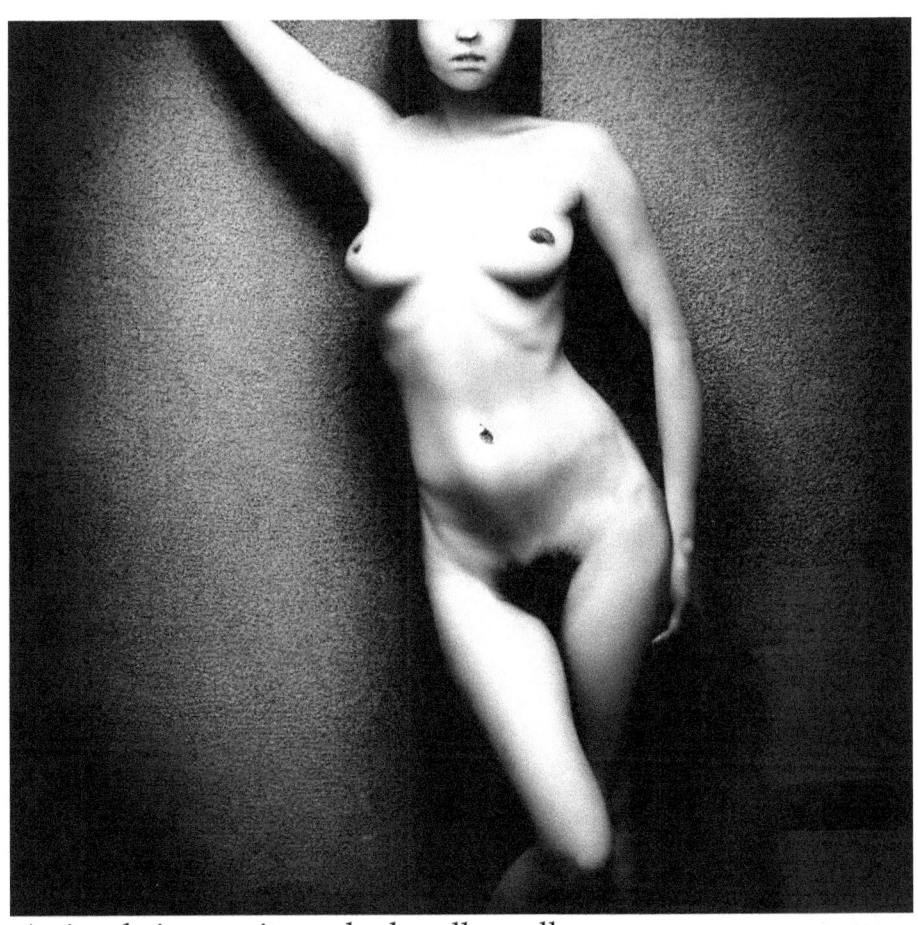
A simple image, it worked really well

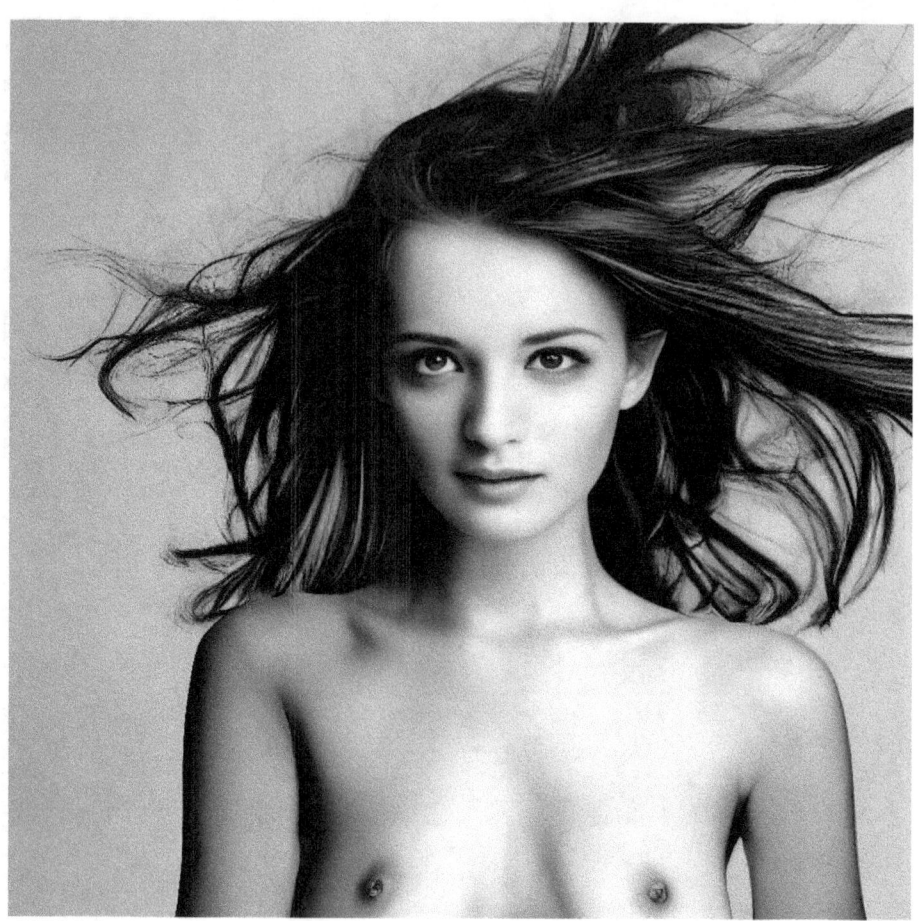
Wild hair

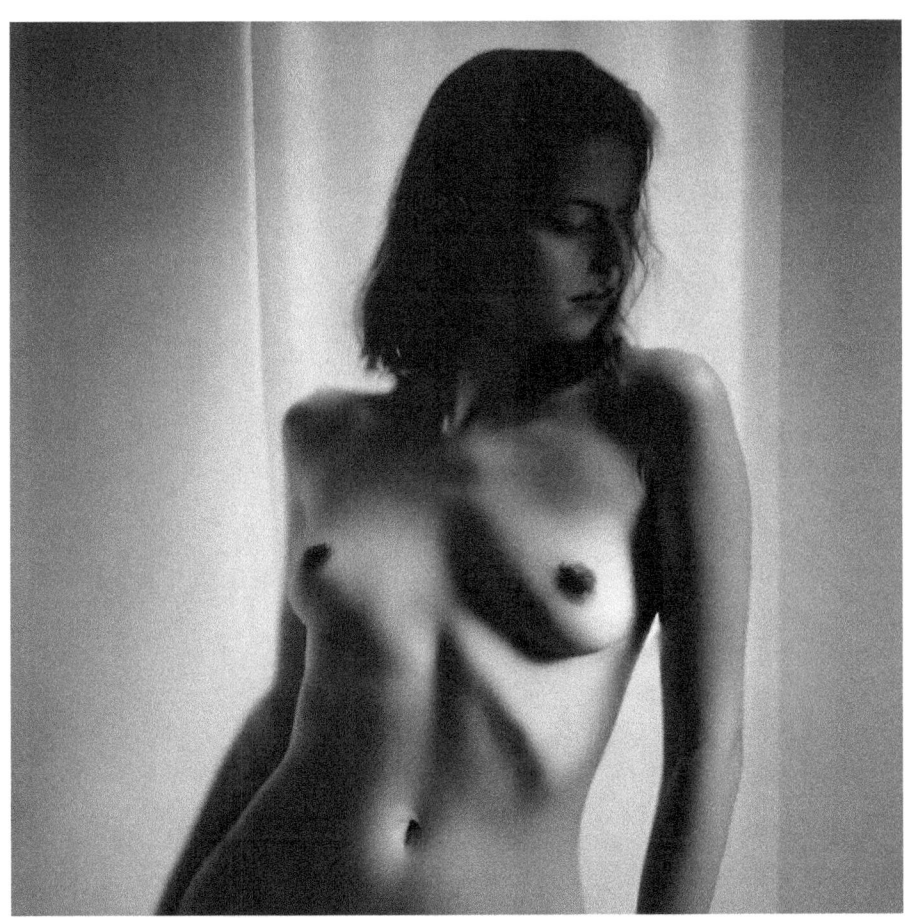
Almost feels pure noir

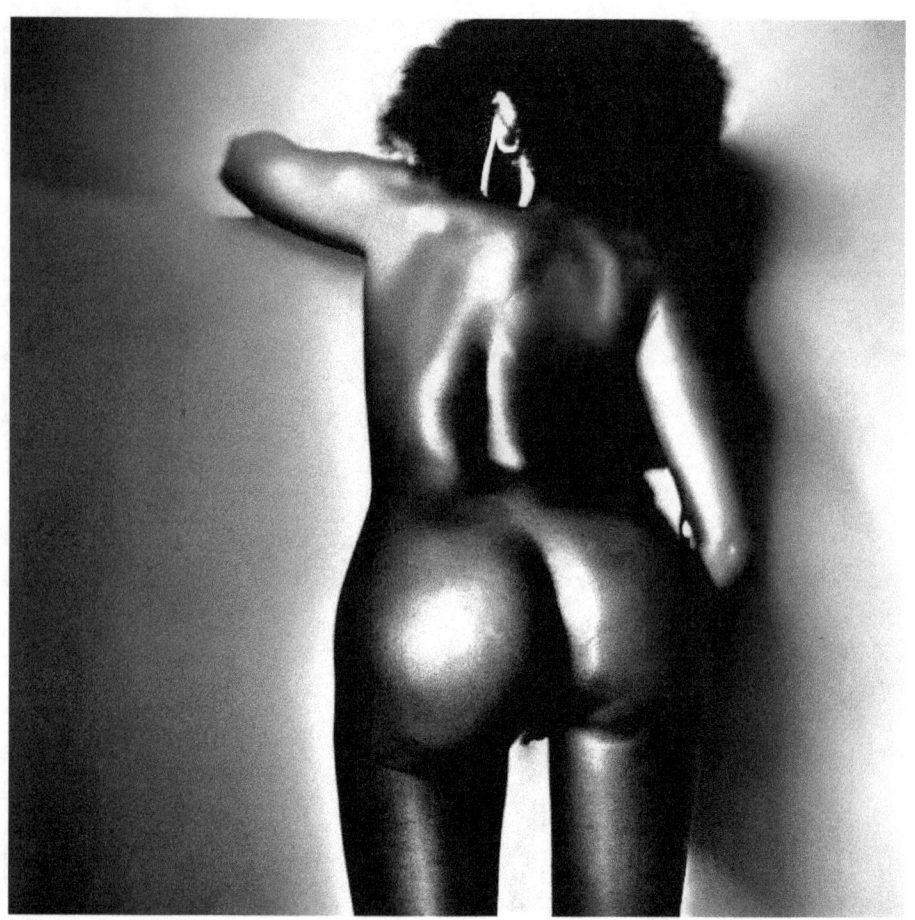

This one feels more explicit than any of the others. The fact that there was no human involved doesn't change that

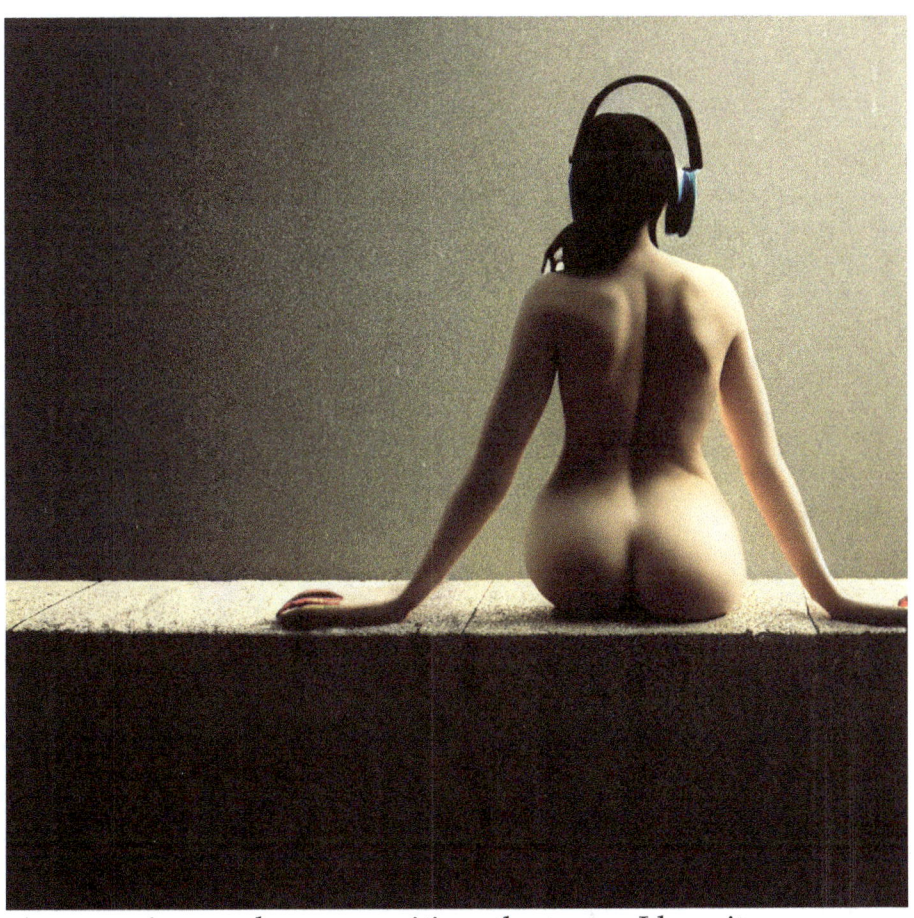

A great picture, the composition, the tones, I love it

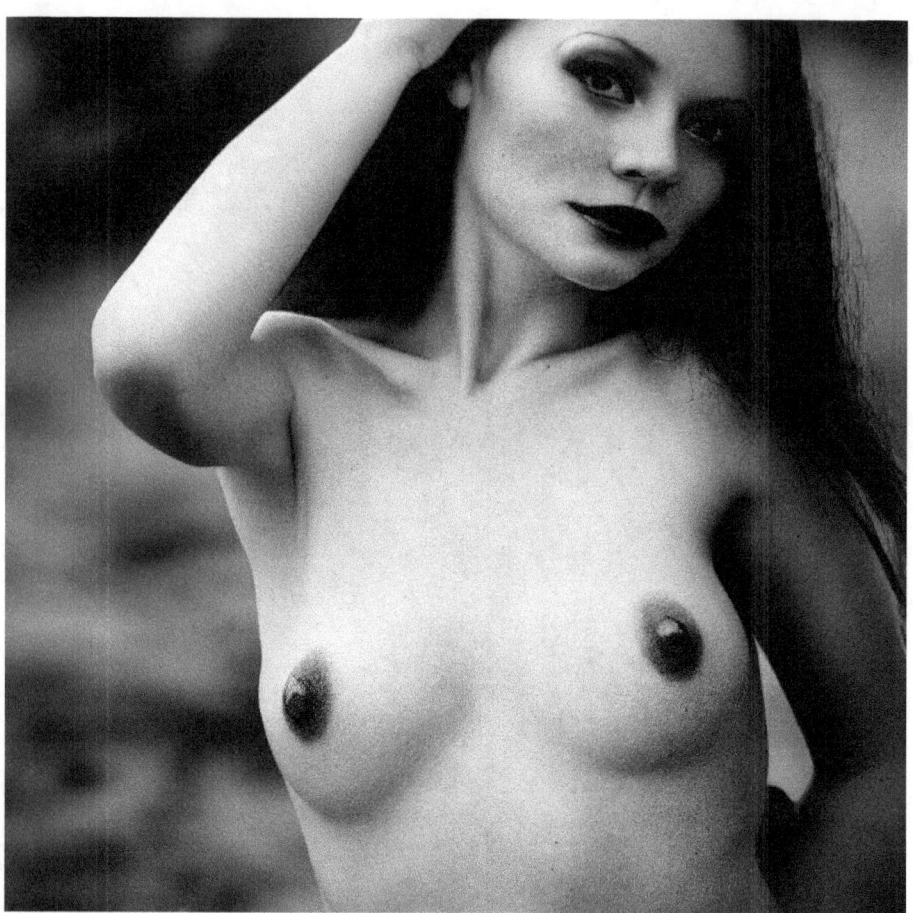

I like the face on this one

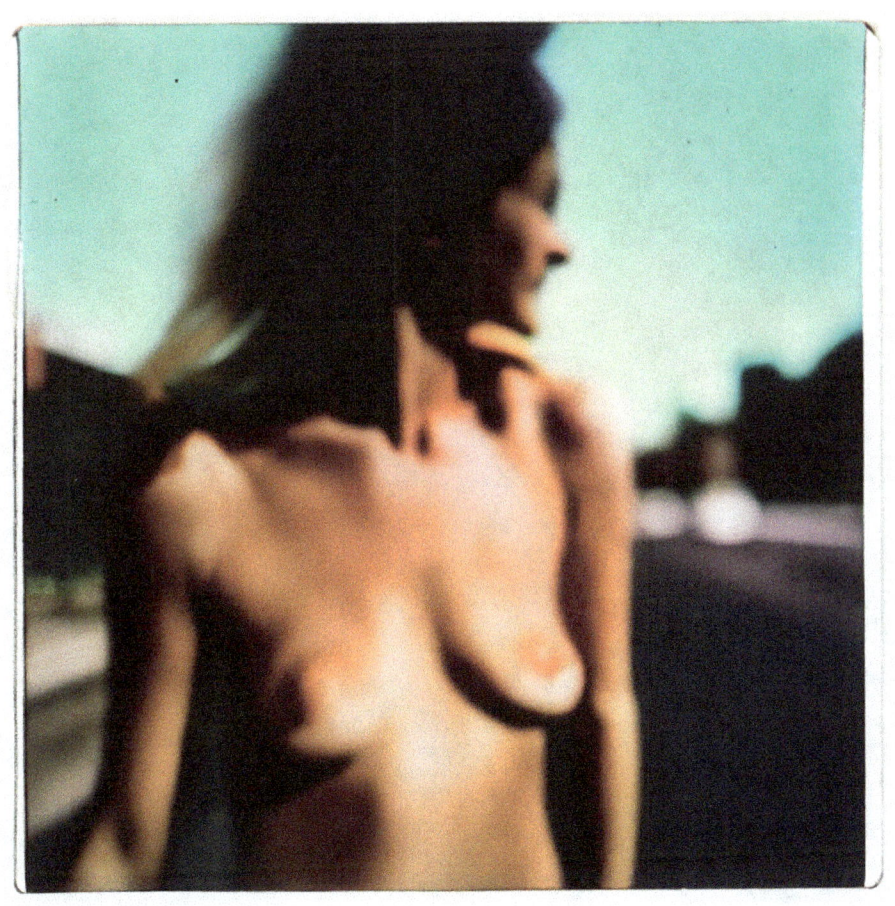

Another case of a photo that benefits from the ambiguity of the polaroid format

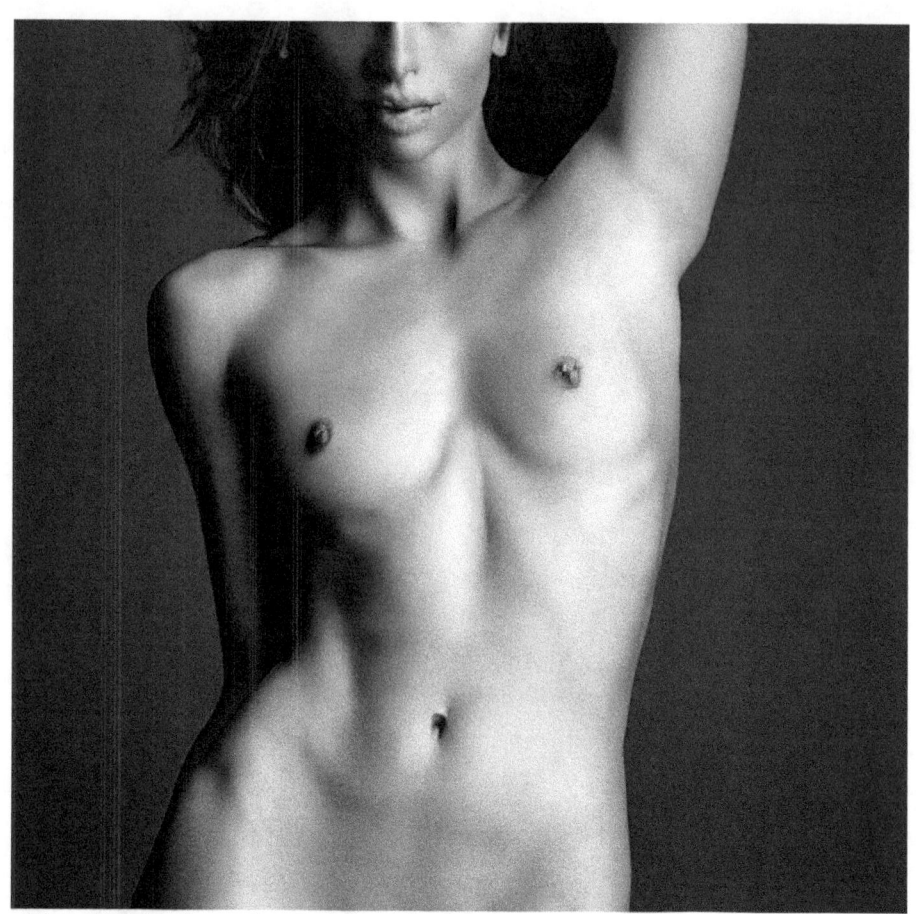

Classic black and white nude

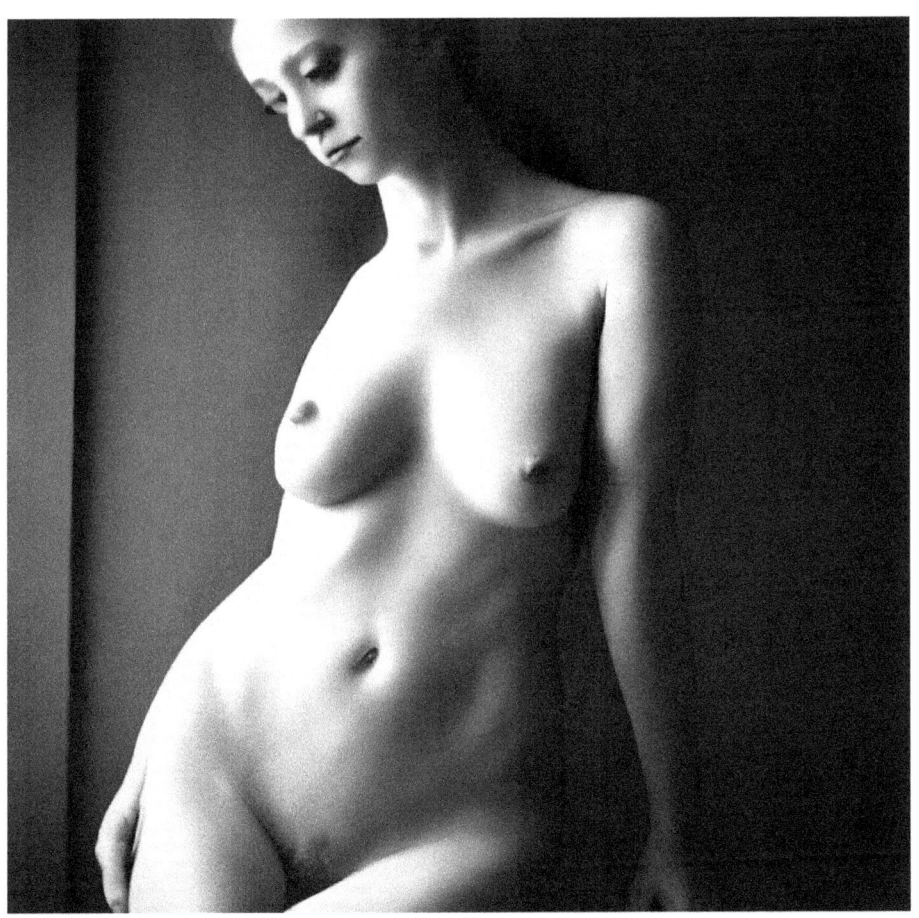
The right shoulder is missing, but otherwise it's a great image

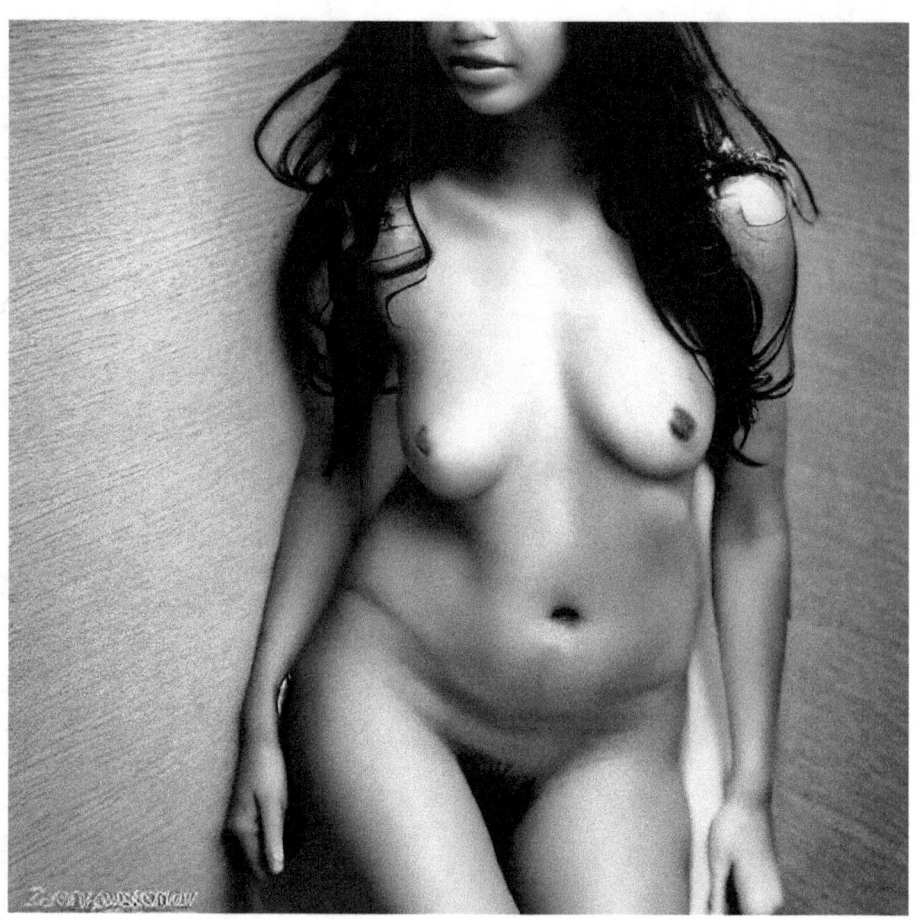

A very real feeling

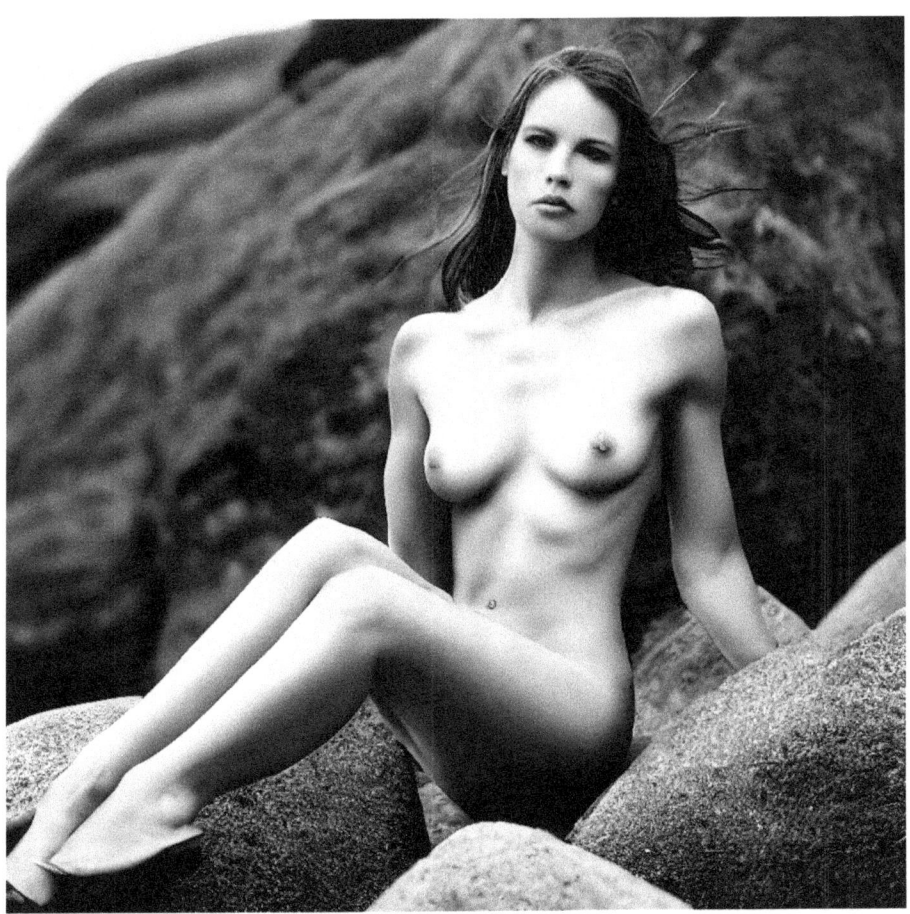

Pretty standard black and white image

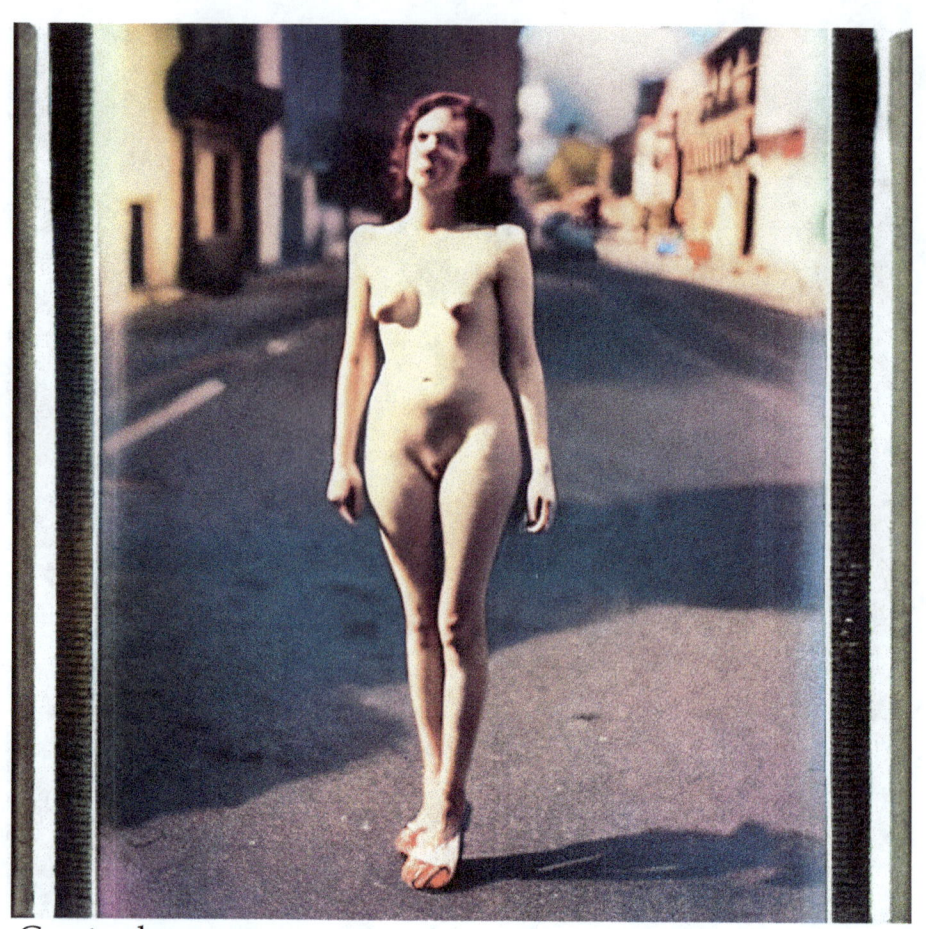
Great colours

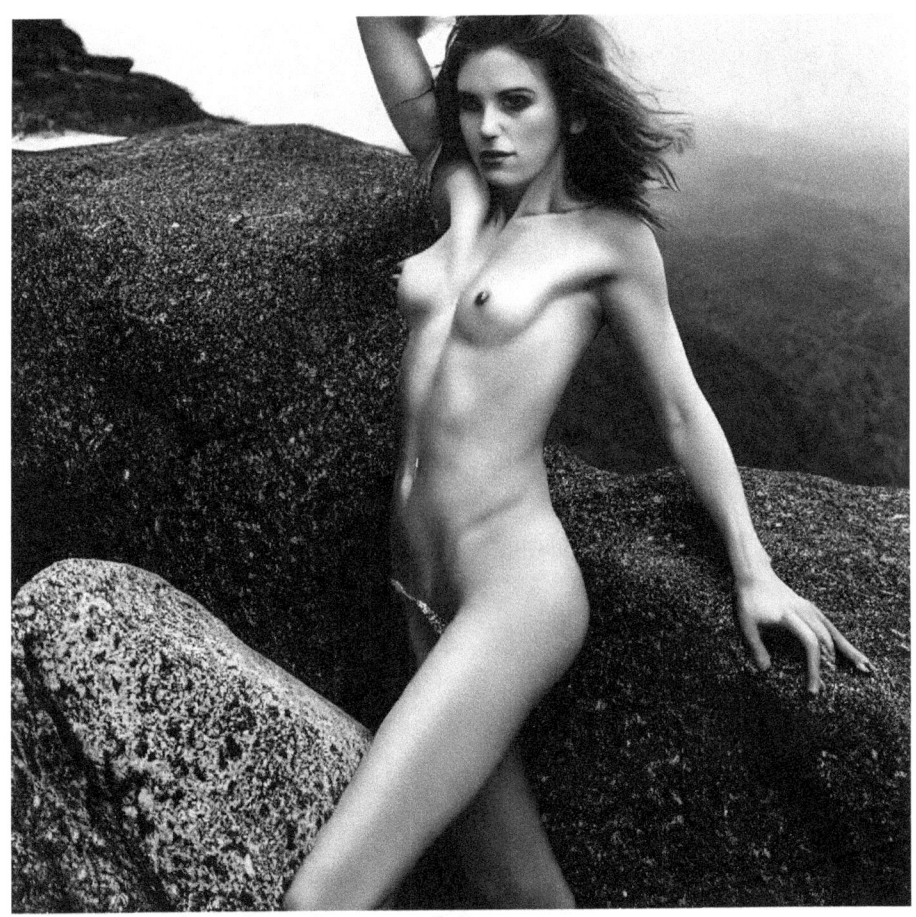
Not sure what the white patch is

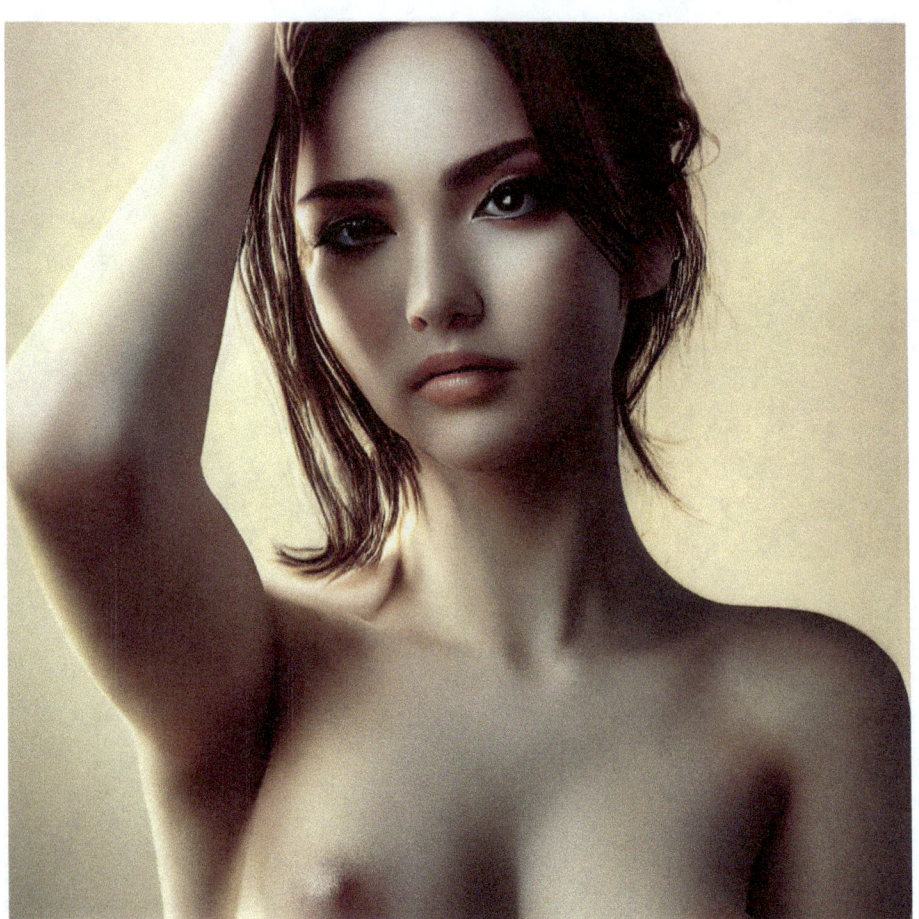
A slick one

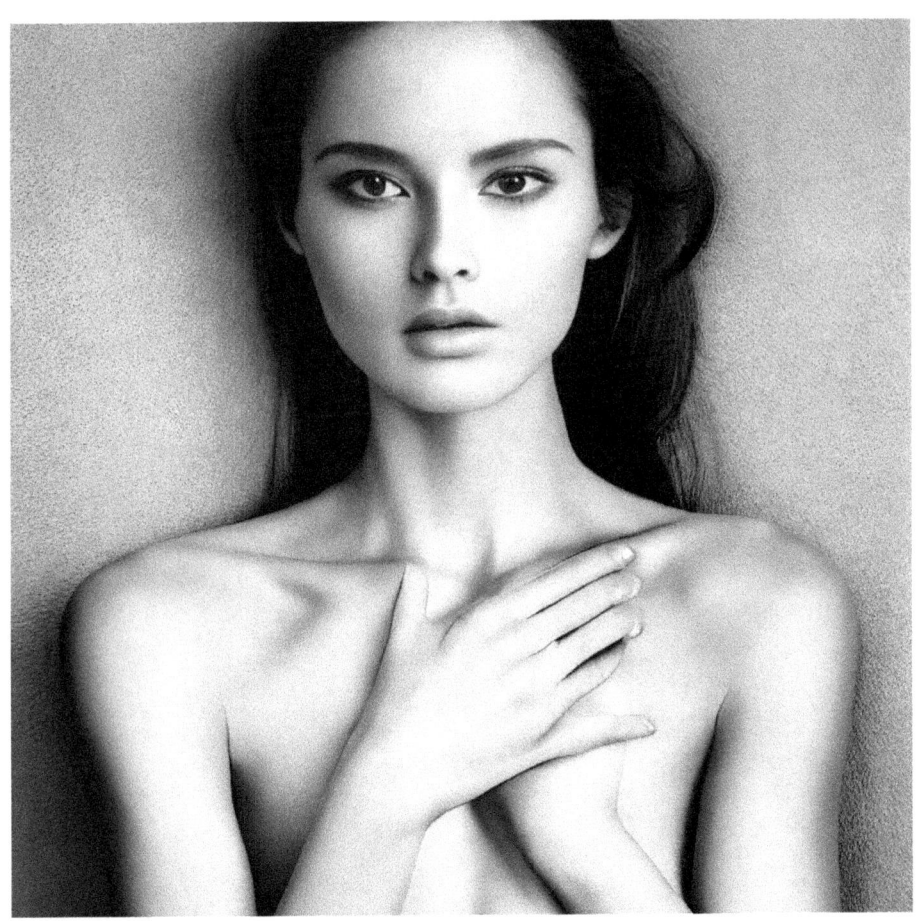
Her left hand is sort of missing

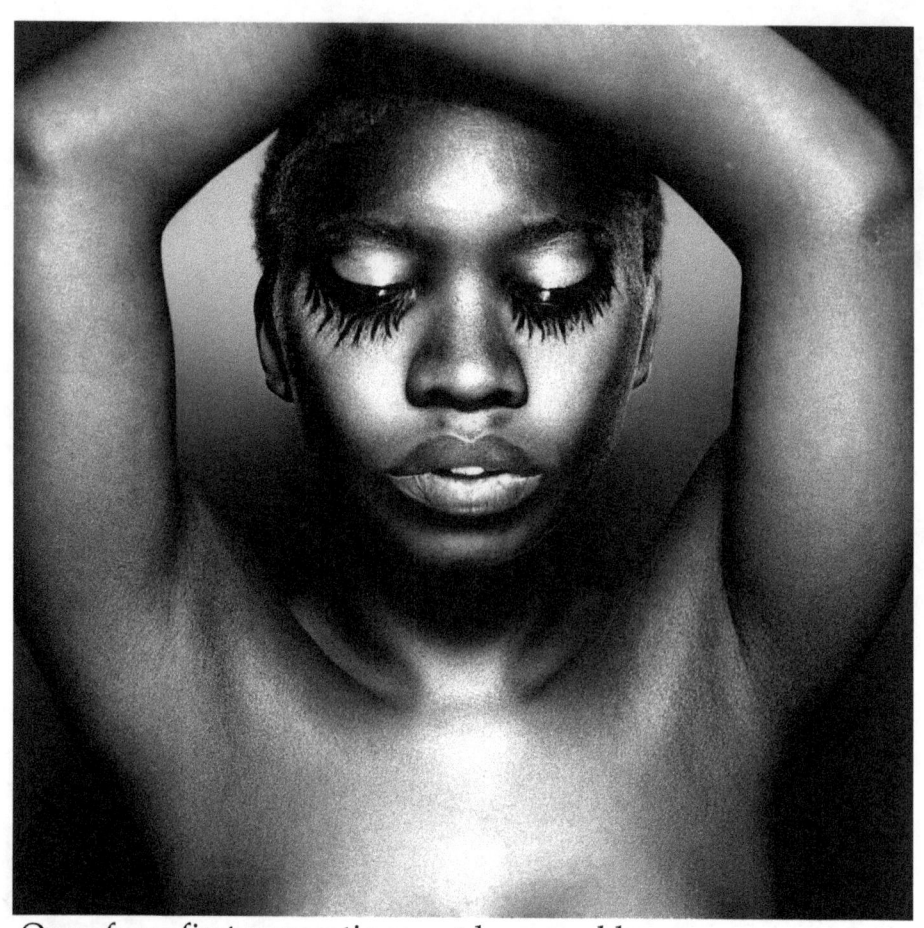
One of our first generations - at least usable ones

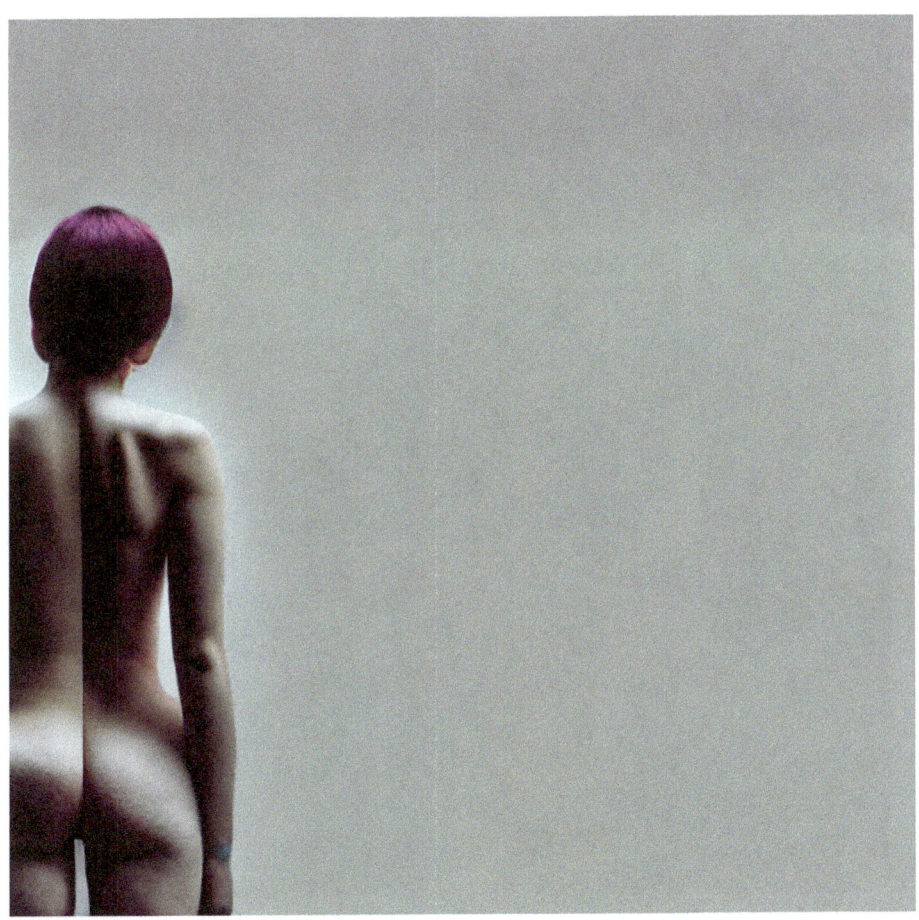
I like the composition here

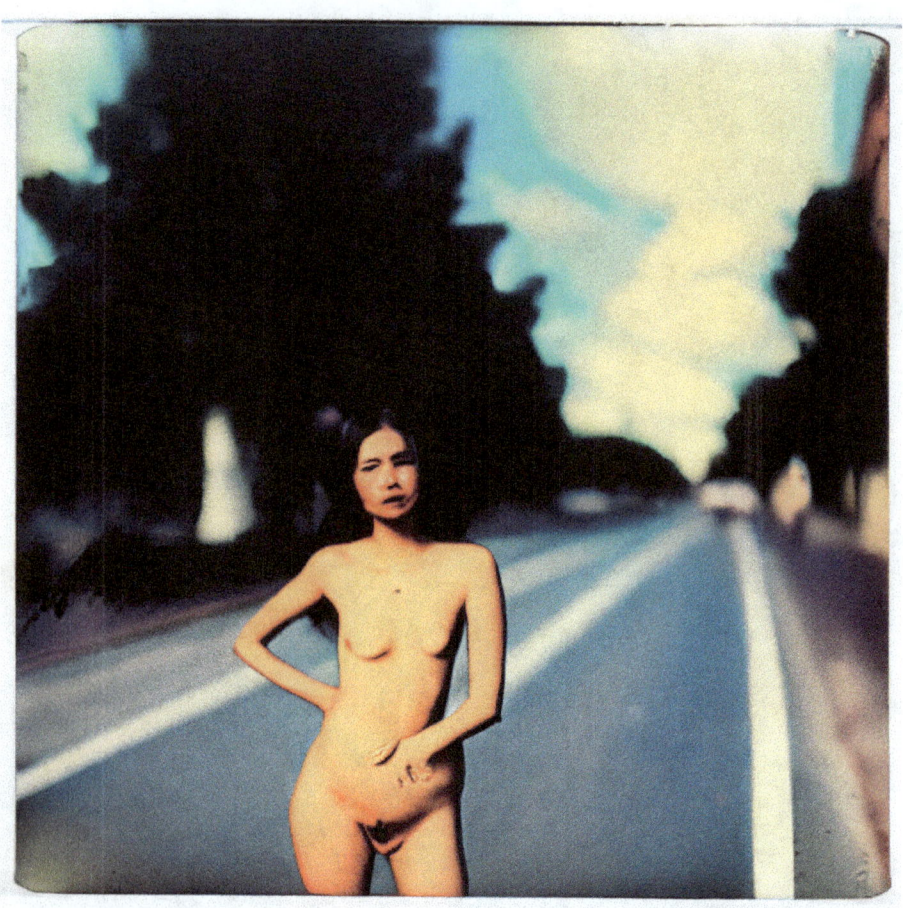
Not one of my favourite polaroids, but it's interesting

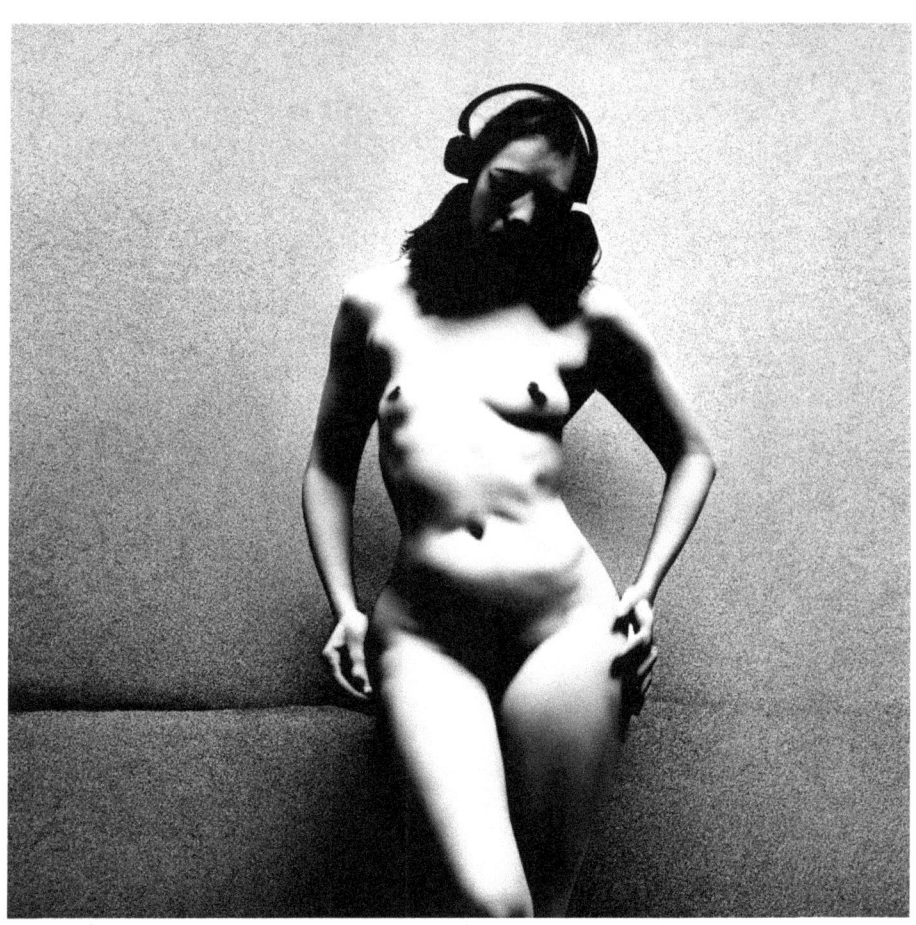

Good tones

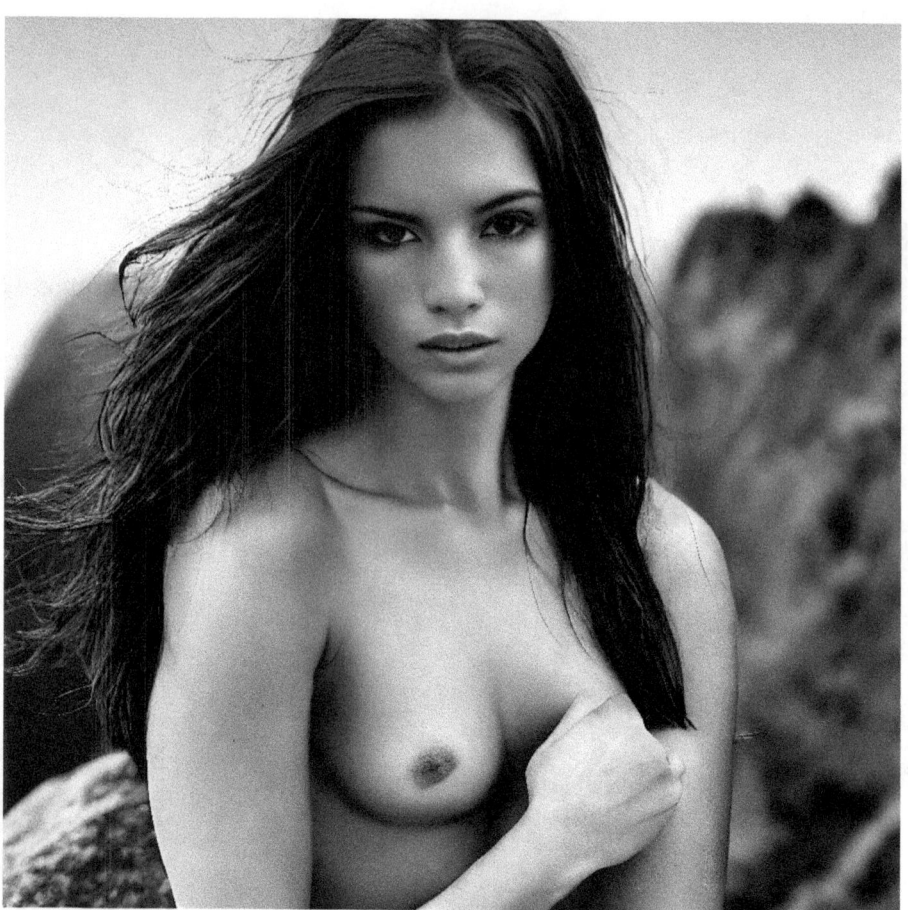
I like the face here

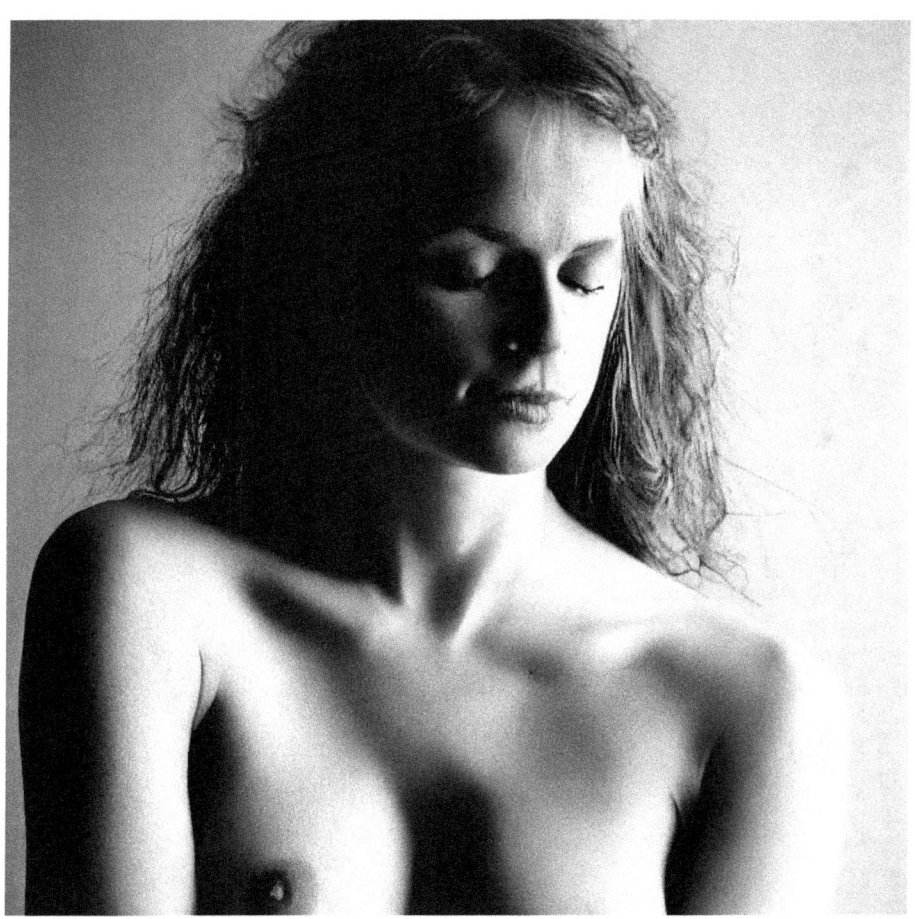

This one feels incredibly real

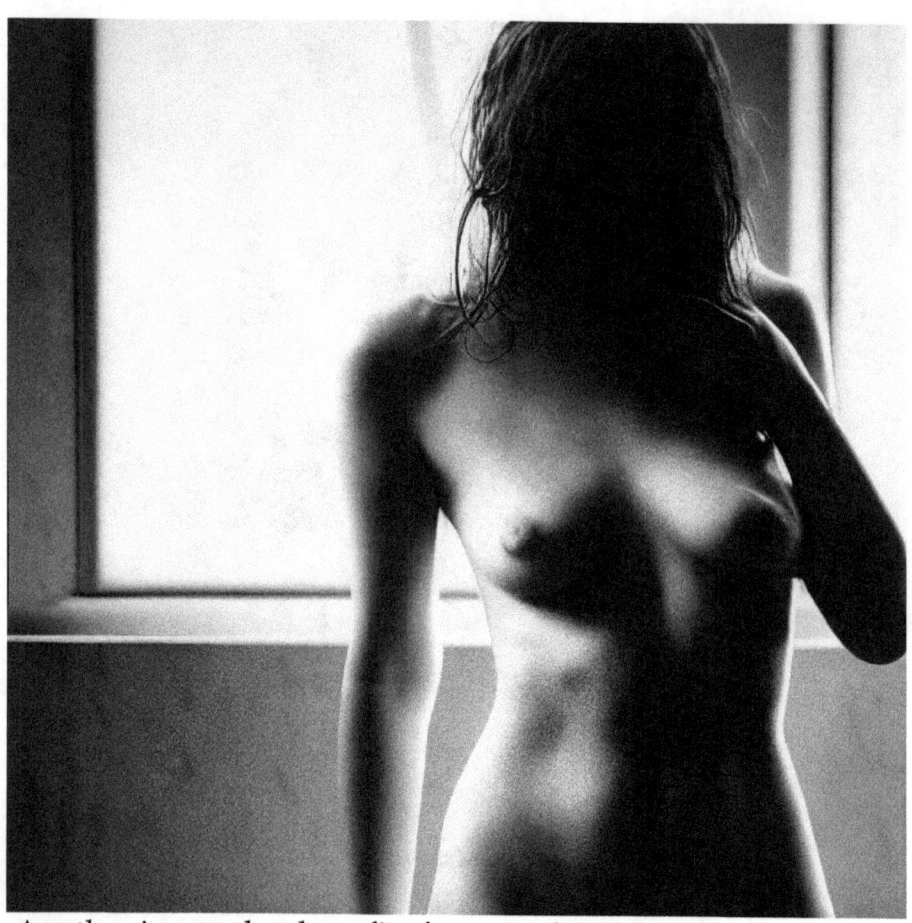
Another image that benefits from not having to render a face

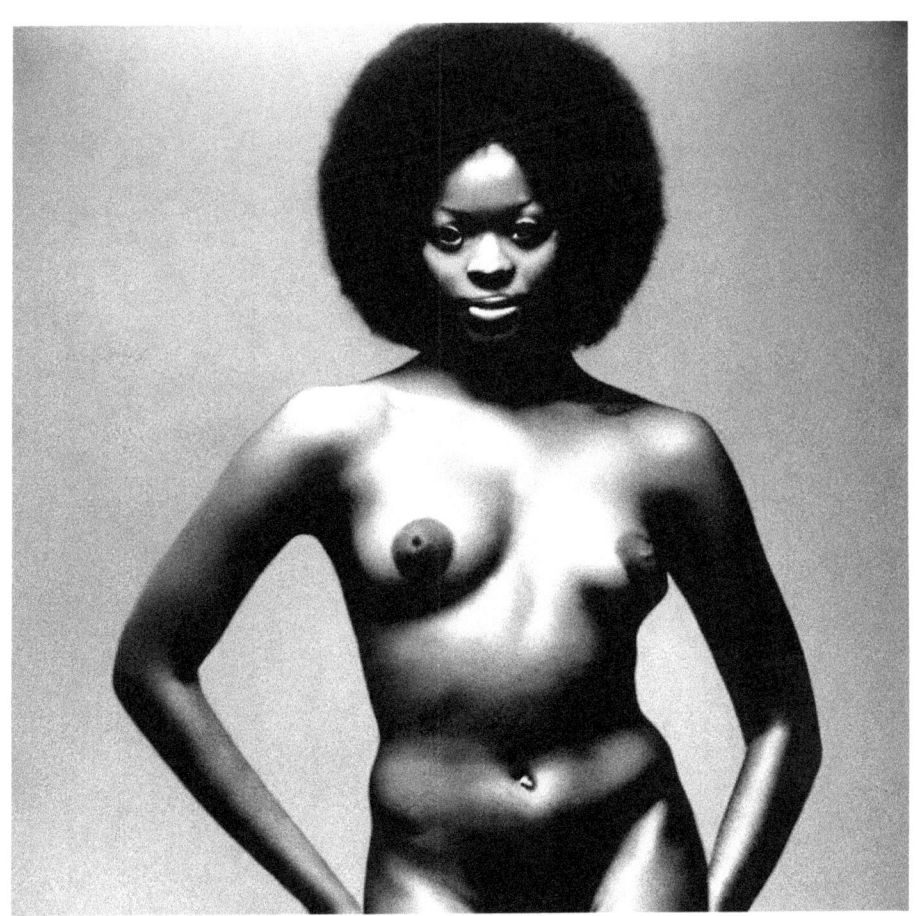
1970's style

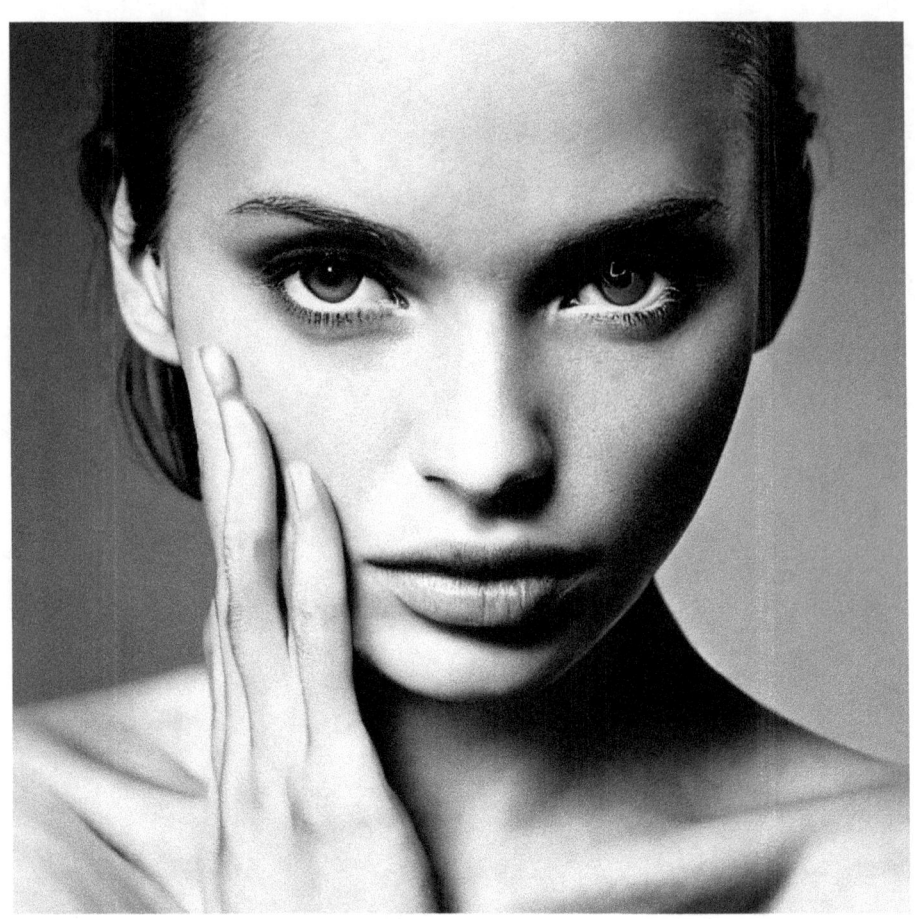
The face here is so real it almost gives me chills

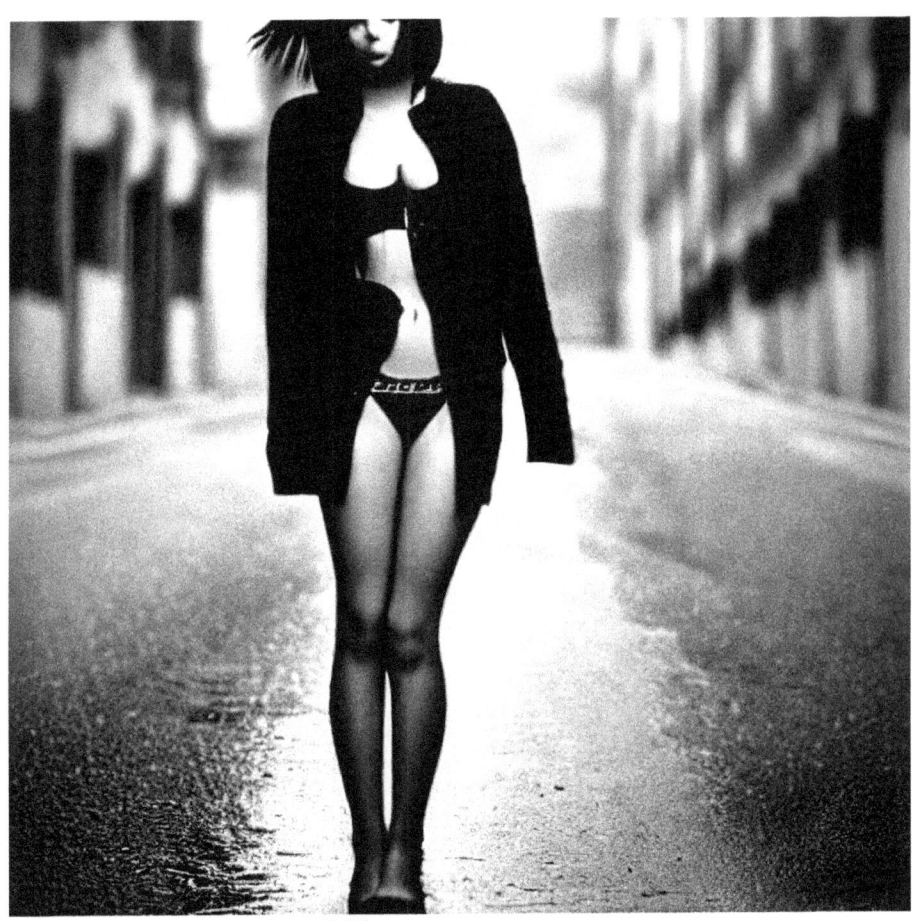

A strange image, but I like it

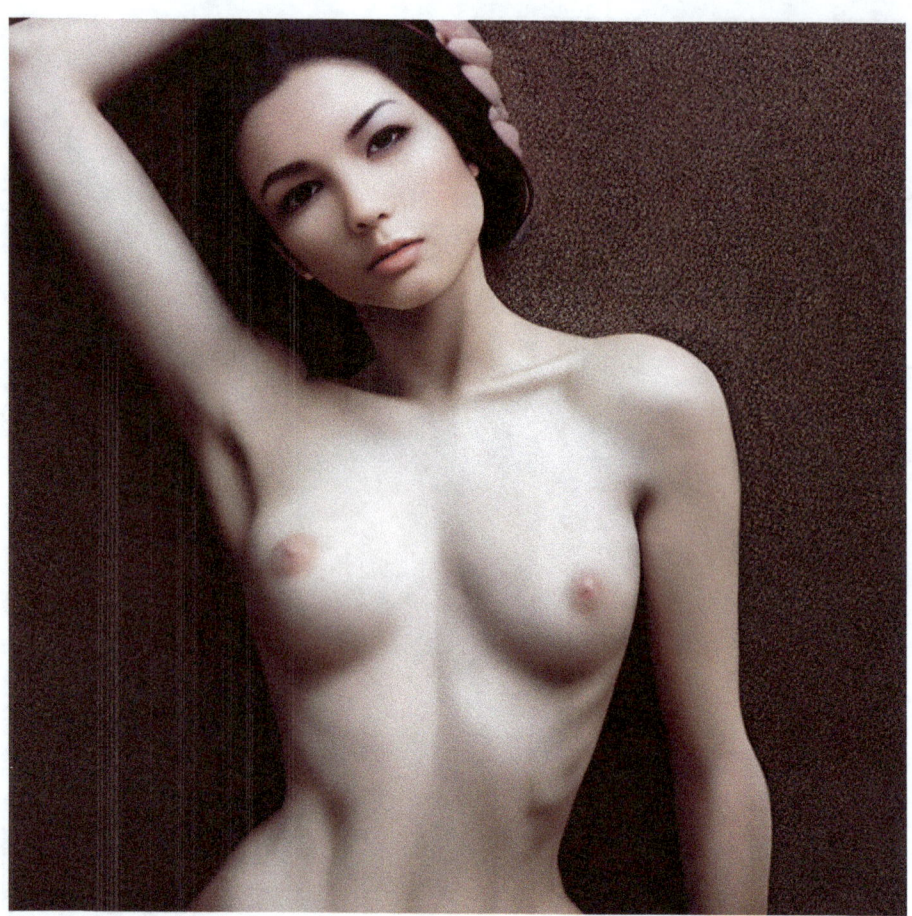
Feels just a little bit off

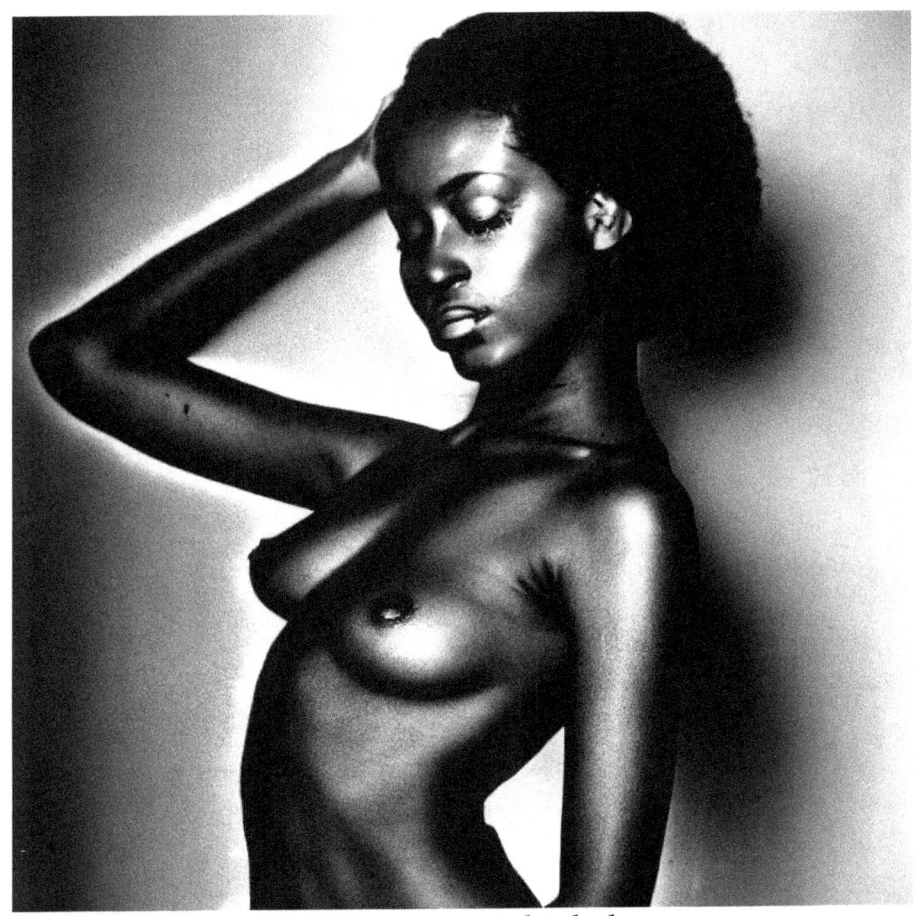

Another relic from another time. I think the prompt mentioned 1970, or at least vintage

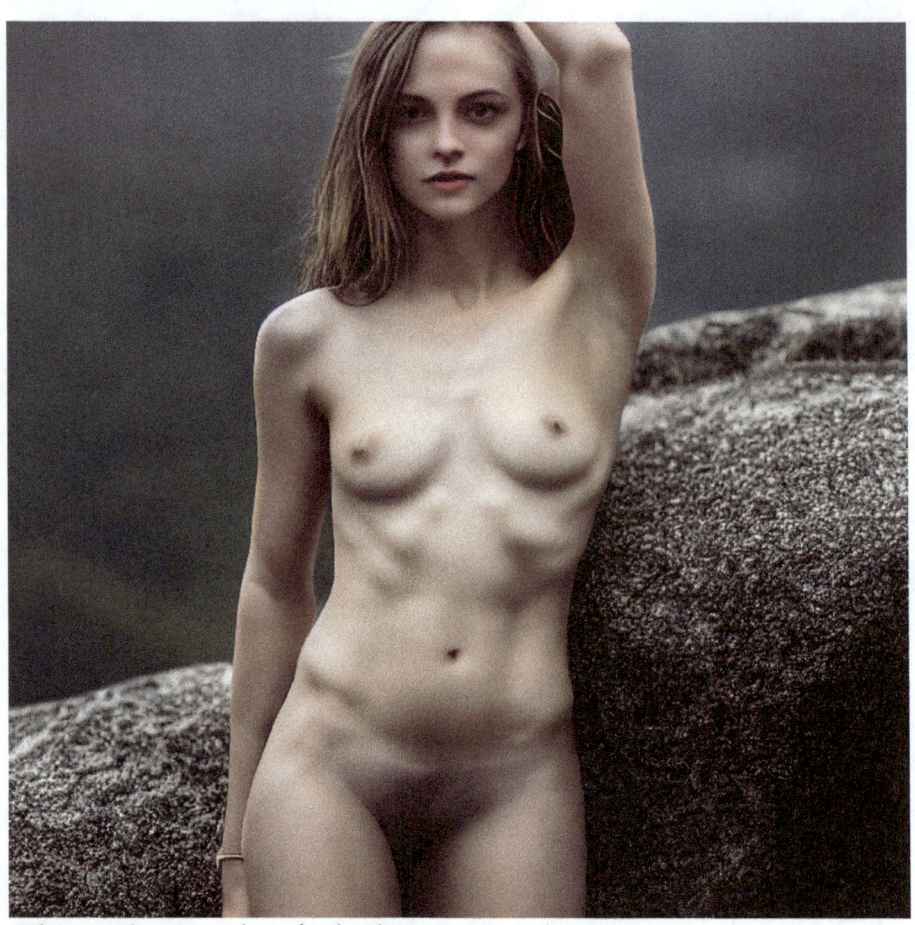
This is the one that feels the most real to me

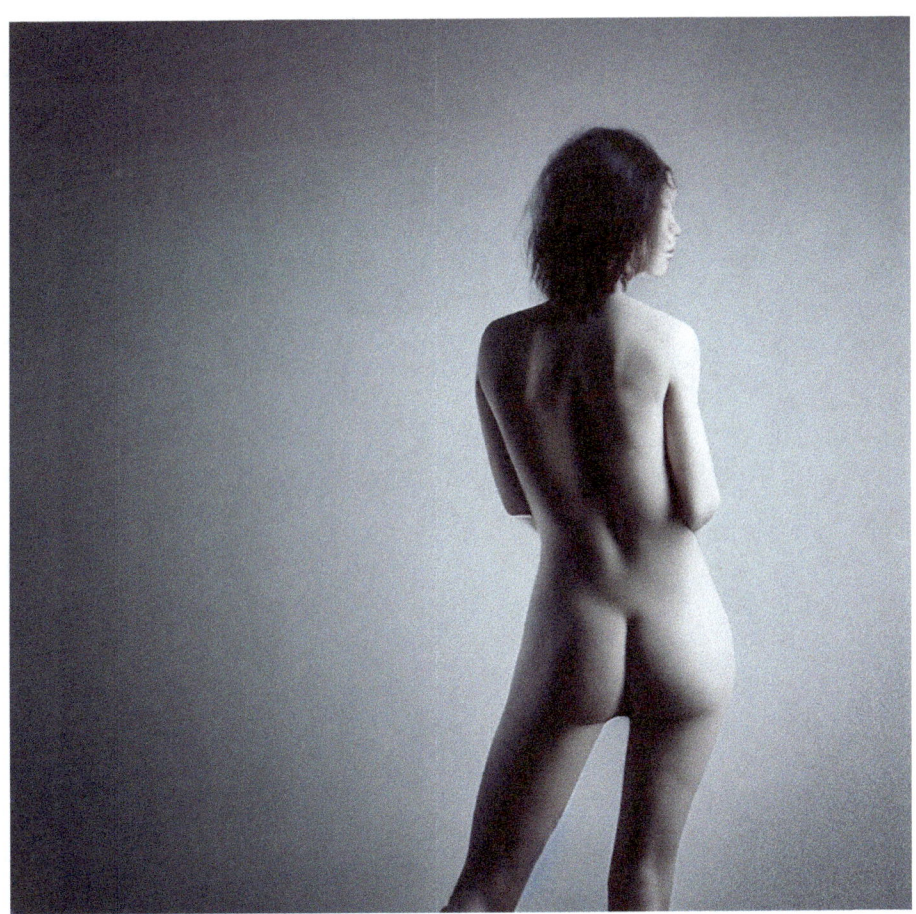
Composition is great

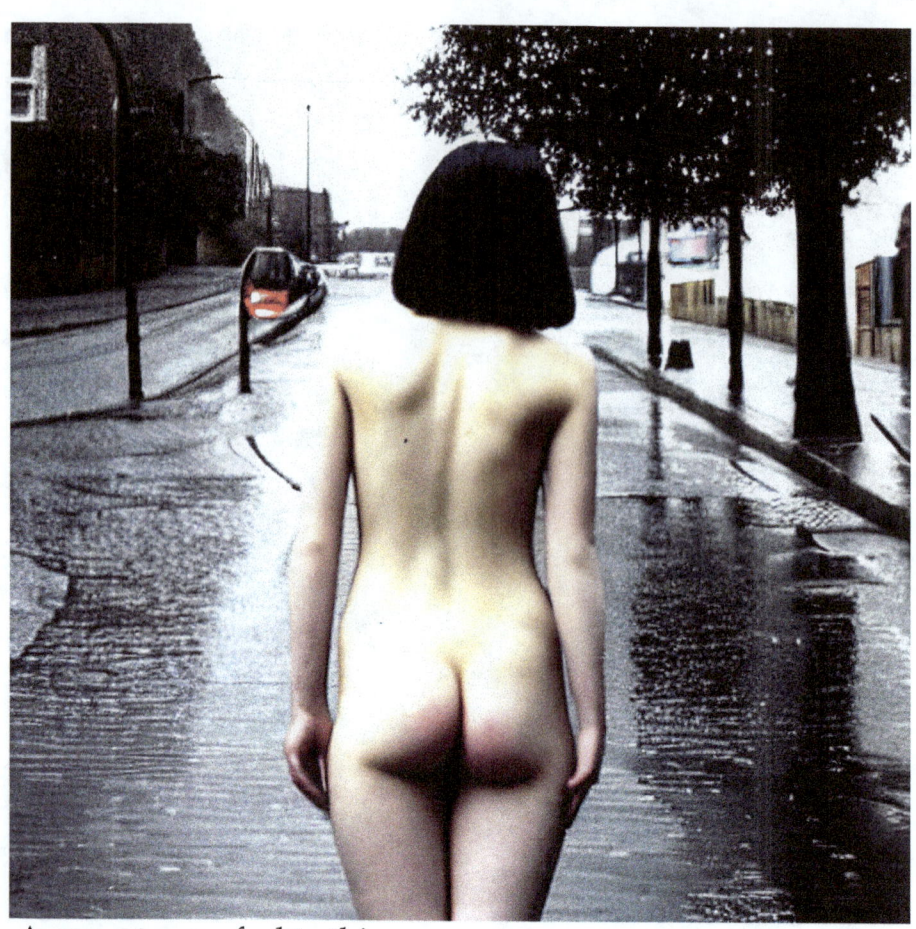
A very strange feel to this one

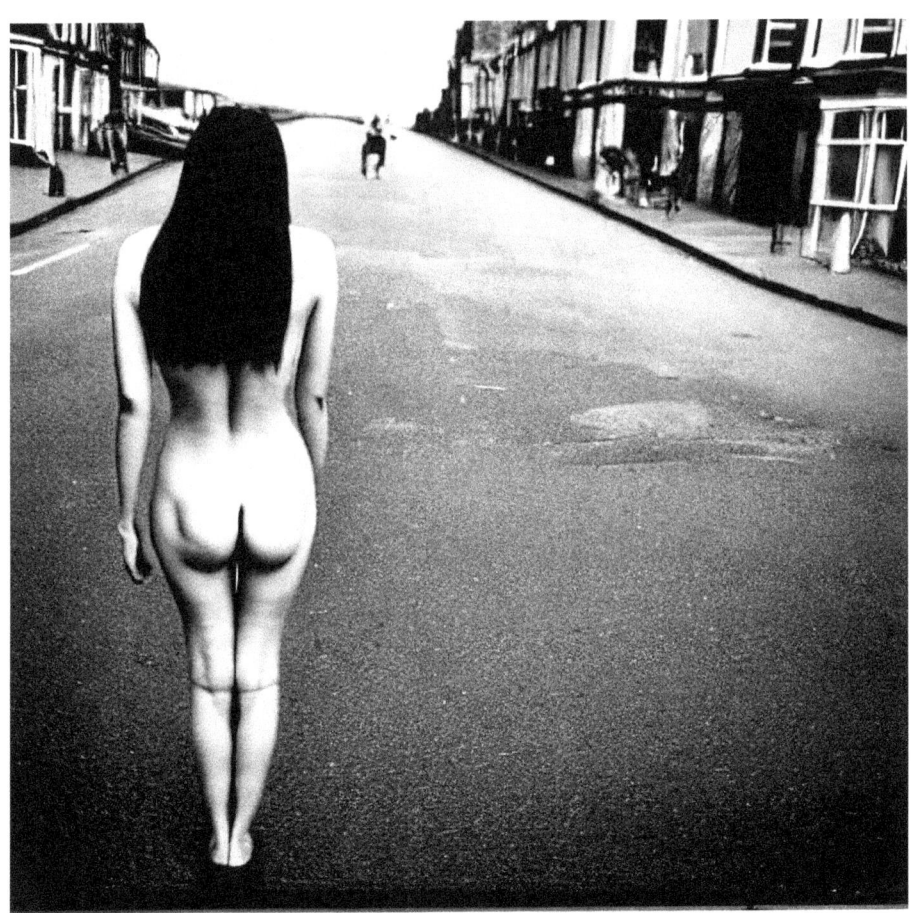
This one feels unsettling

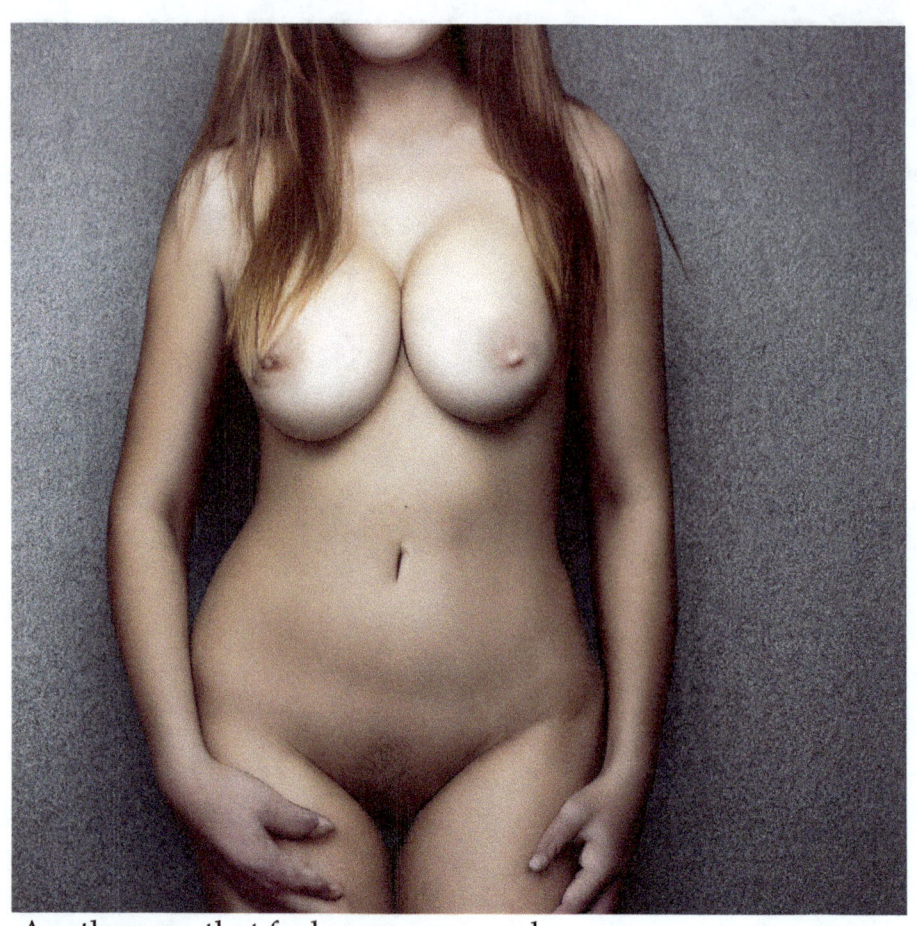
Another one that feels very very real

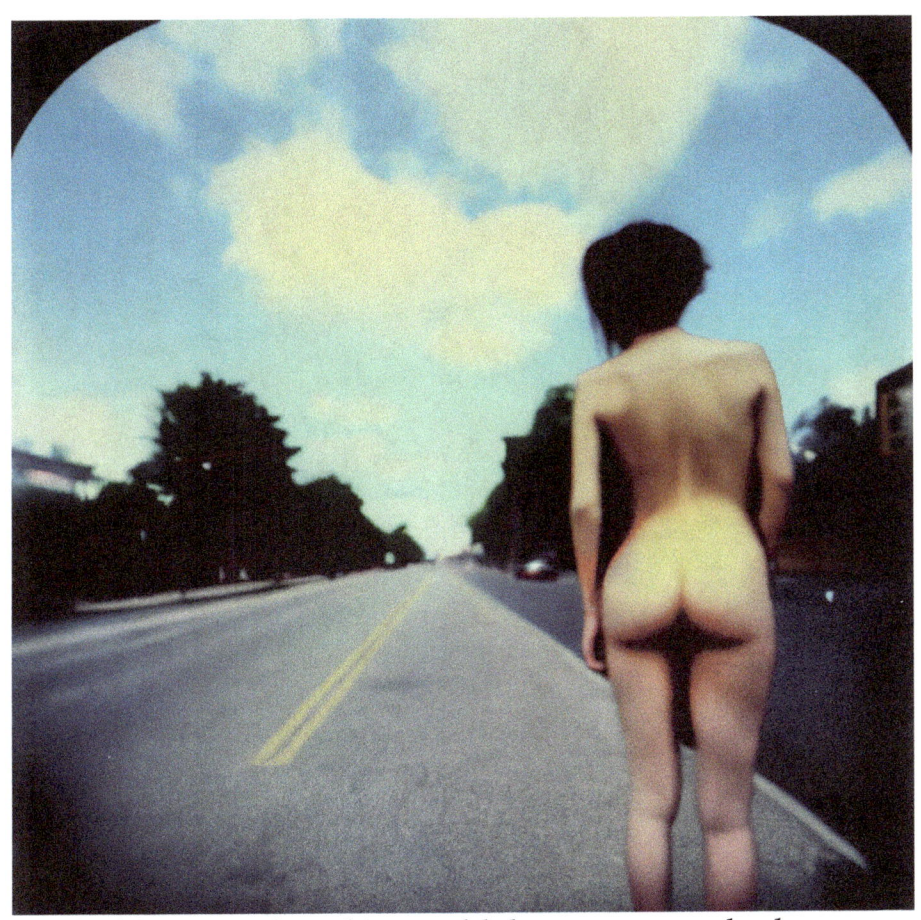
Looks like it was found in an old drawer at a yard sale

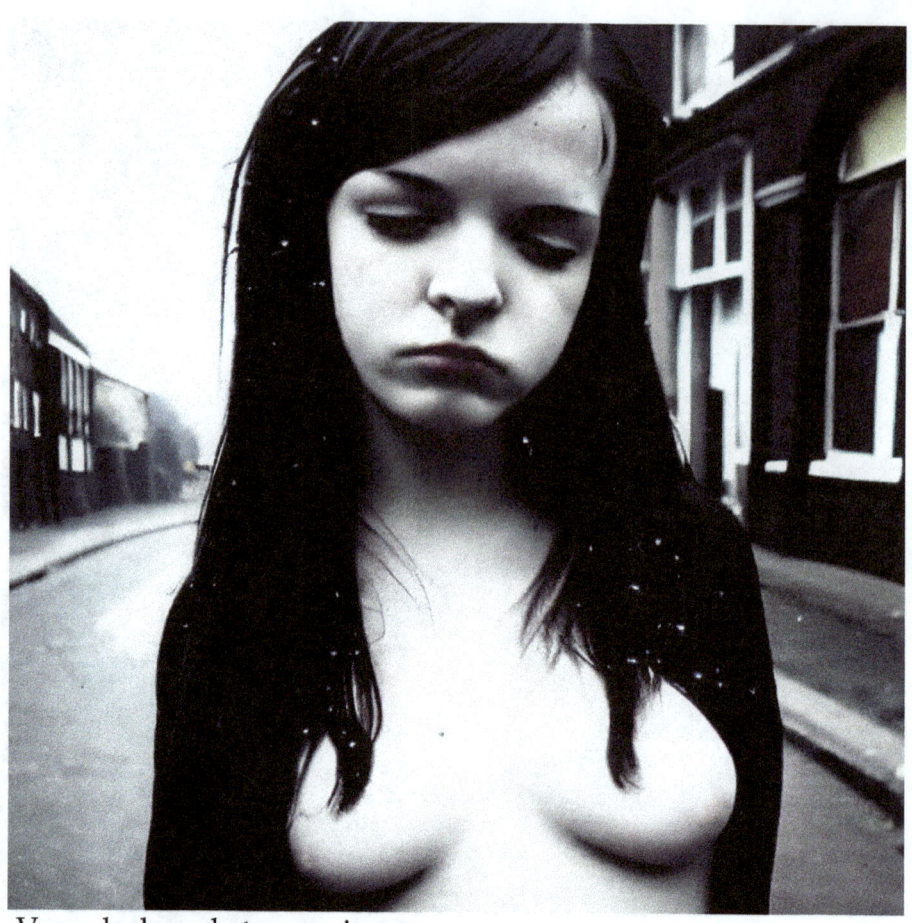
Very dark and strange image

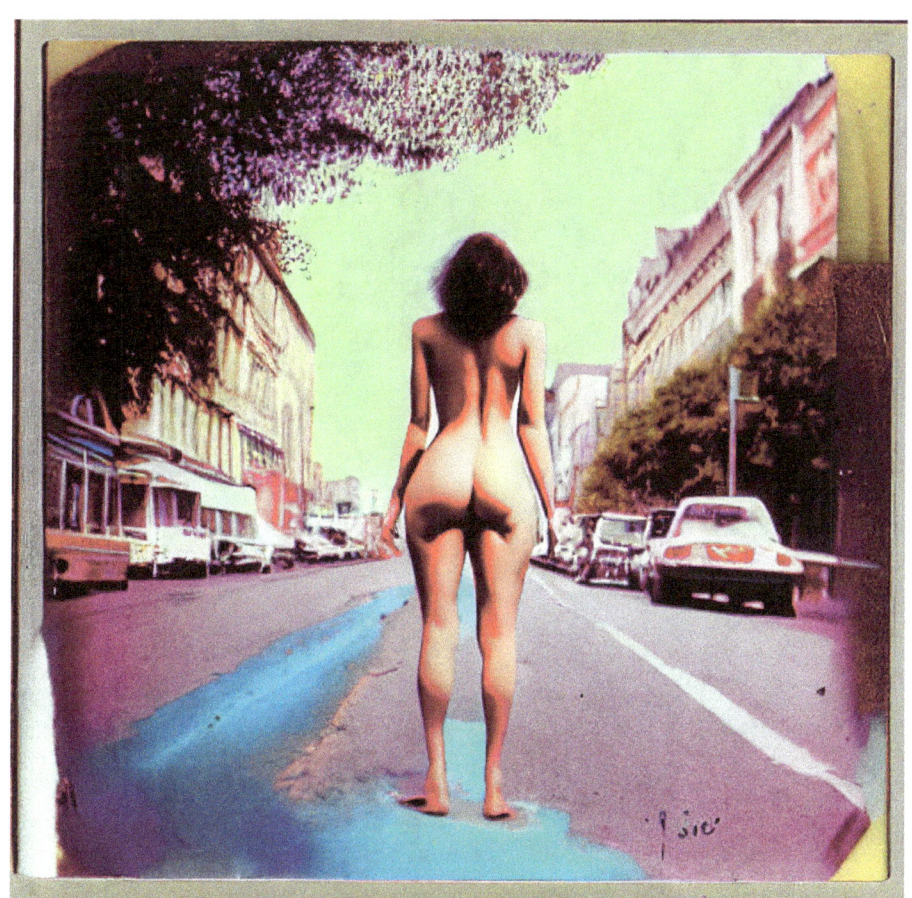

Trippy colours

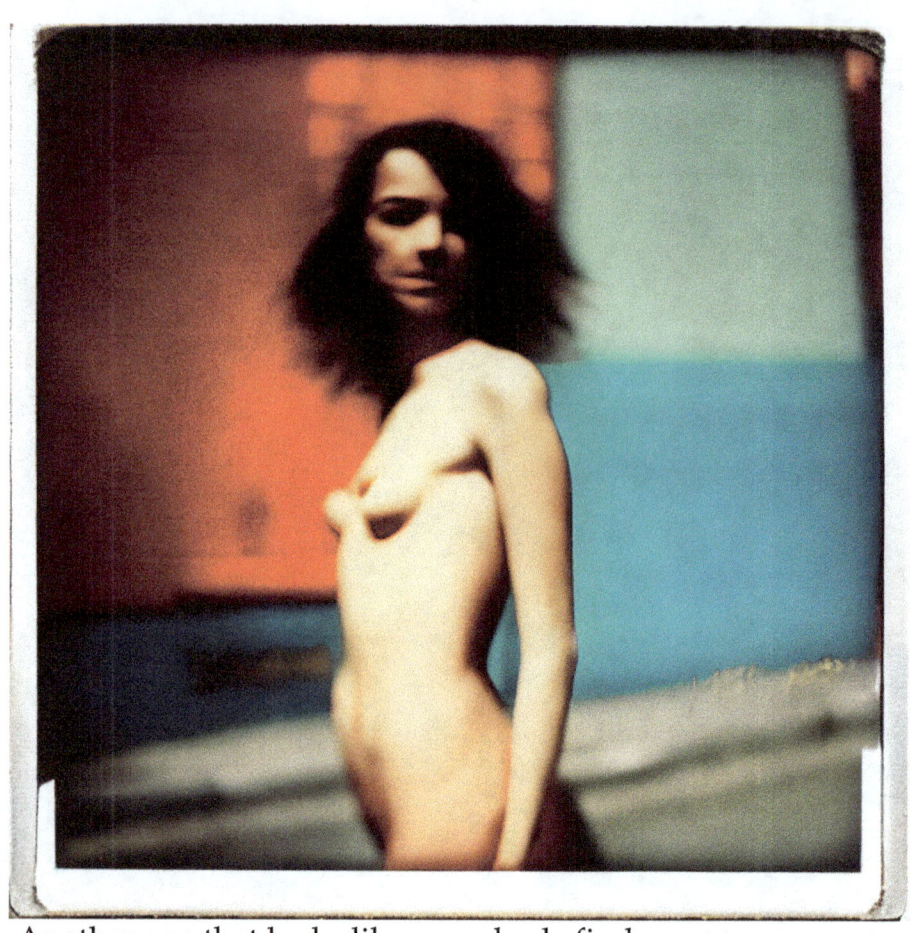
Another one that looks like a yard sale find

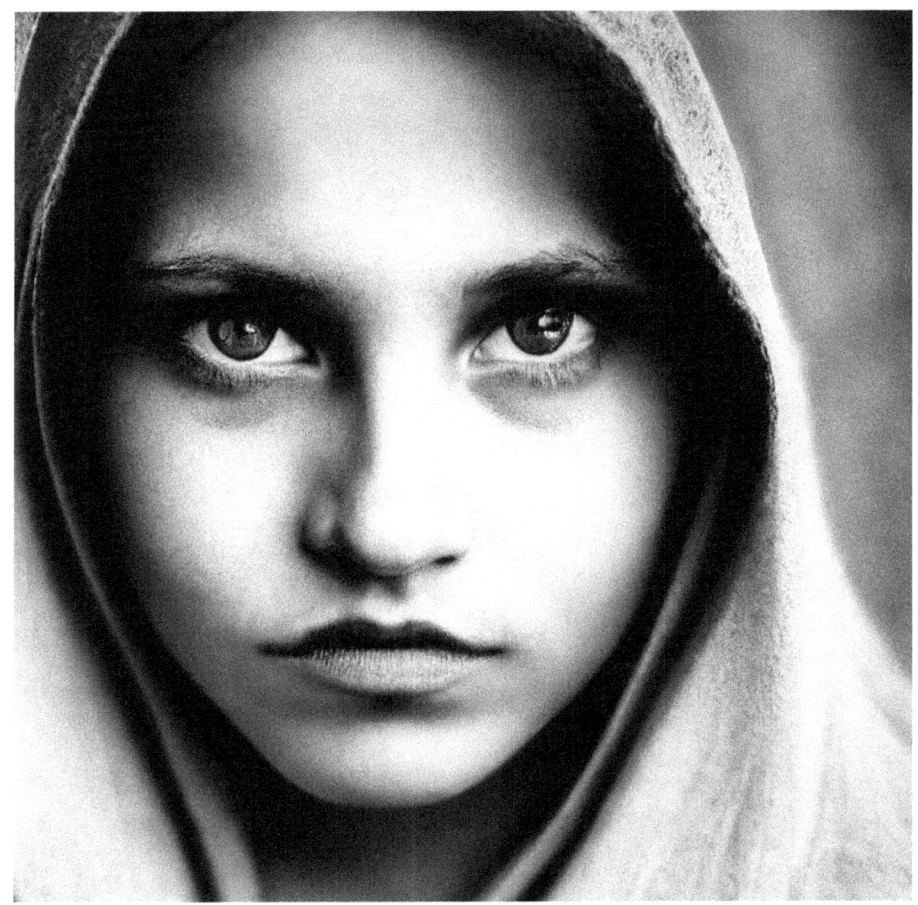

Amazing eyes - it doesn't quite fit the theme of the book, but I had to include it

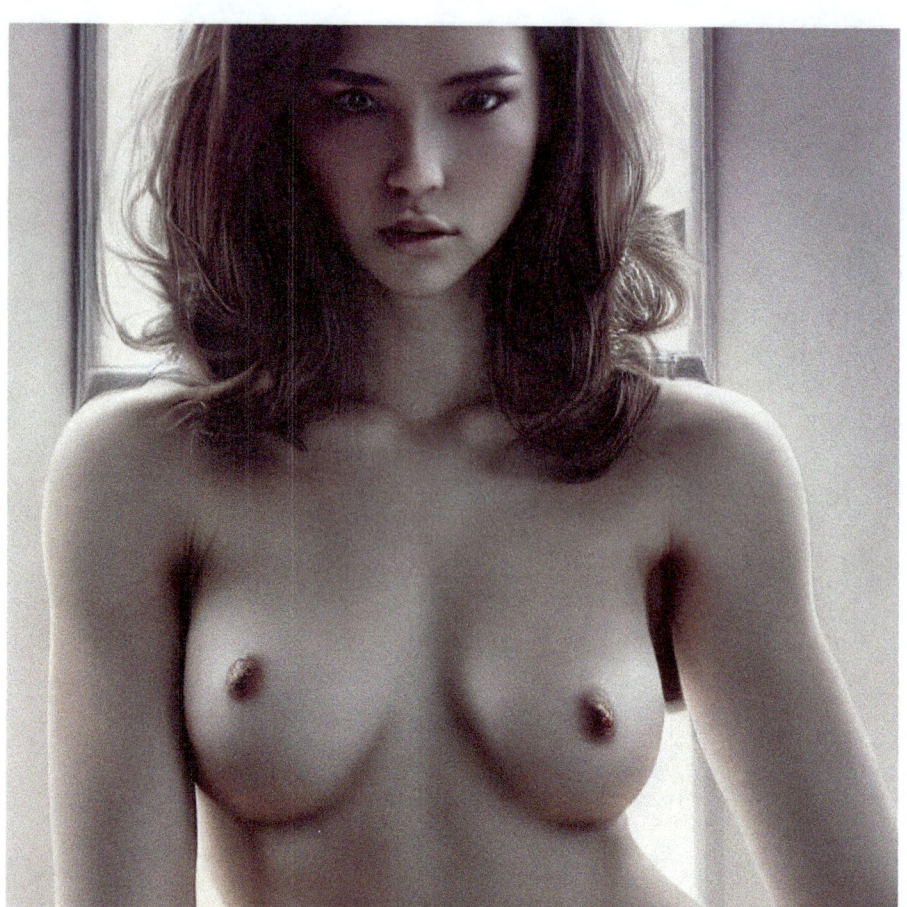
Intense look

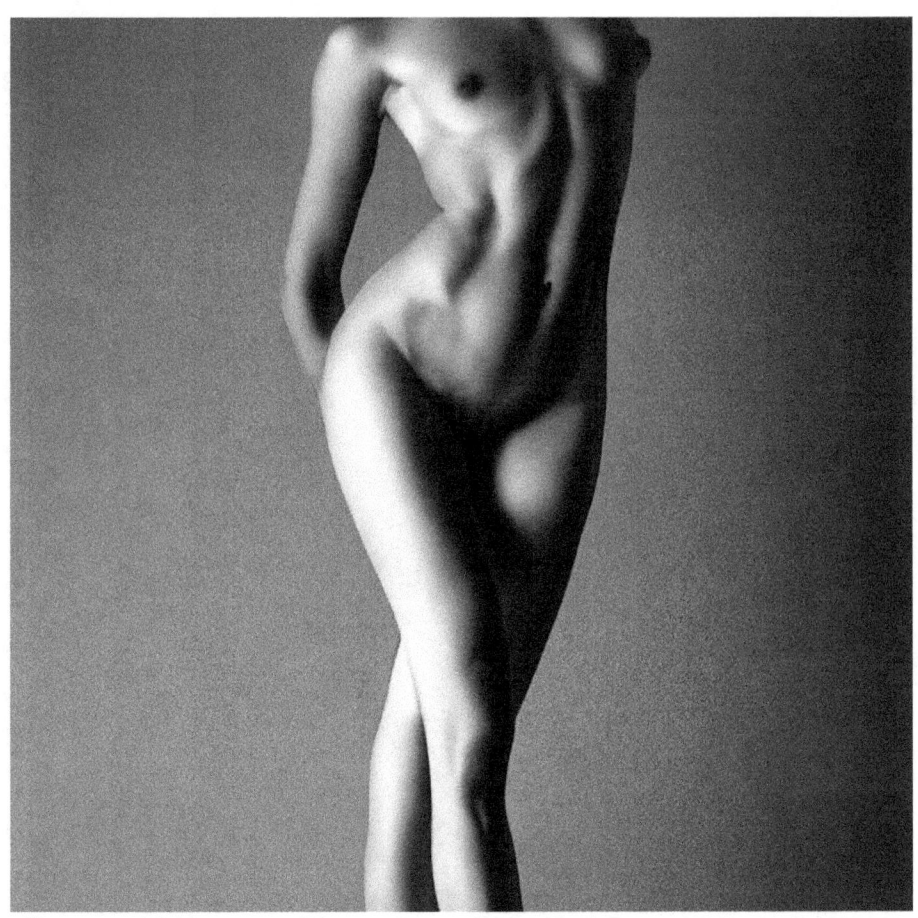
Composition, tone, it's a great picture

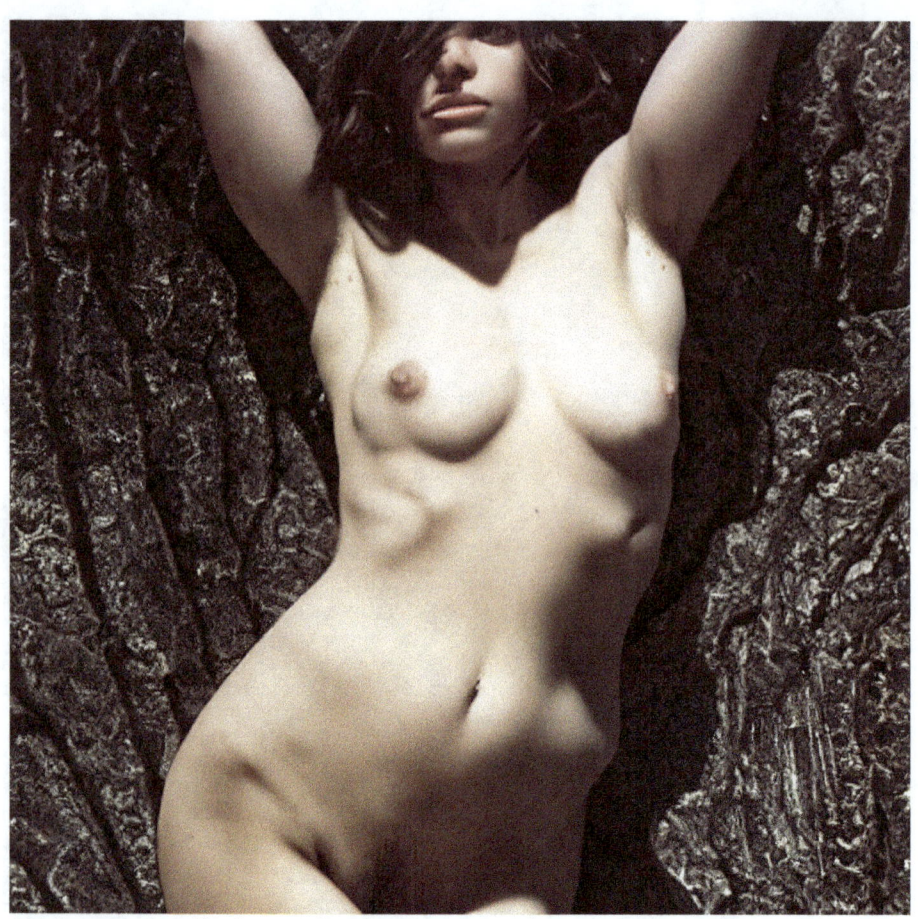
This one is all about the background textures

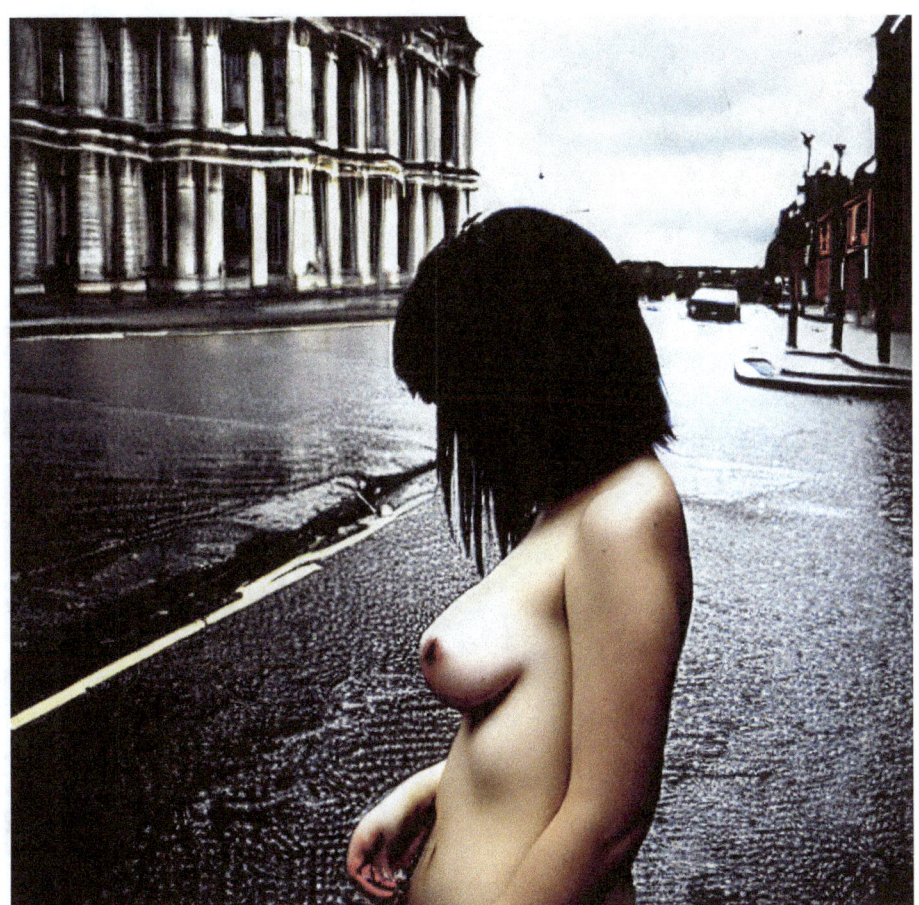
A decent shot

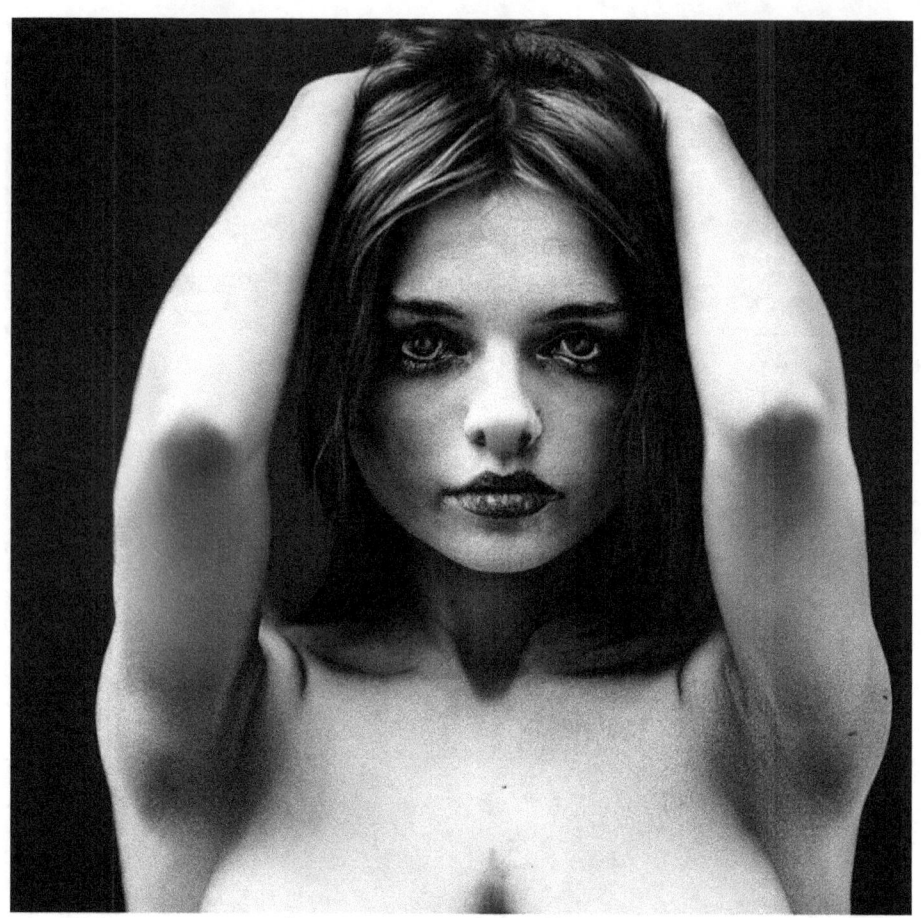
An intense stare - the eyes are a bit off

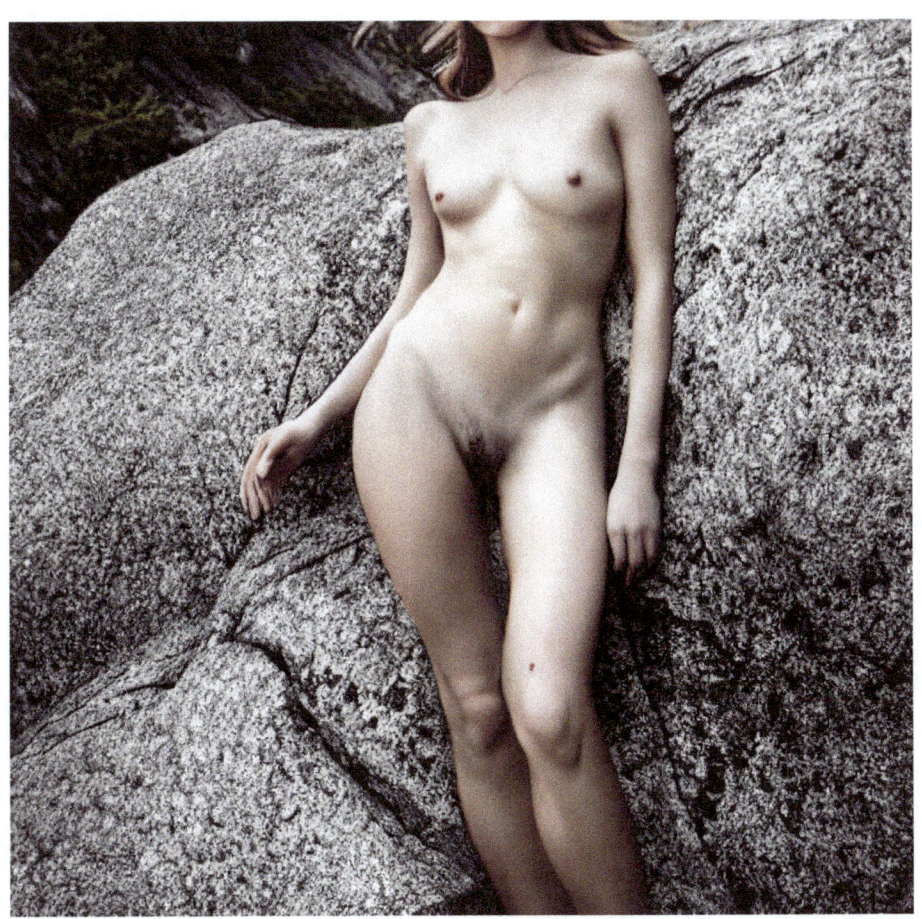
This one worked really well

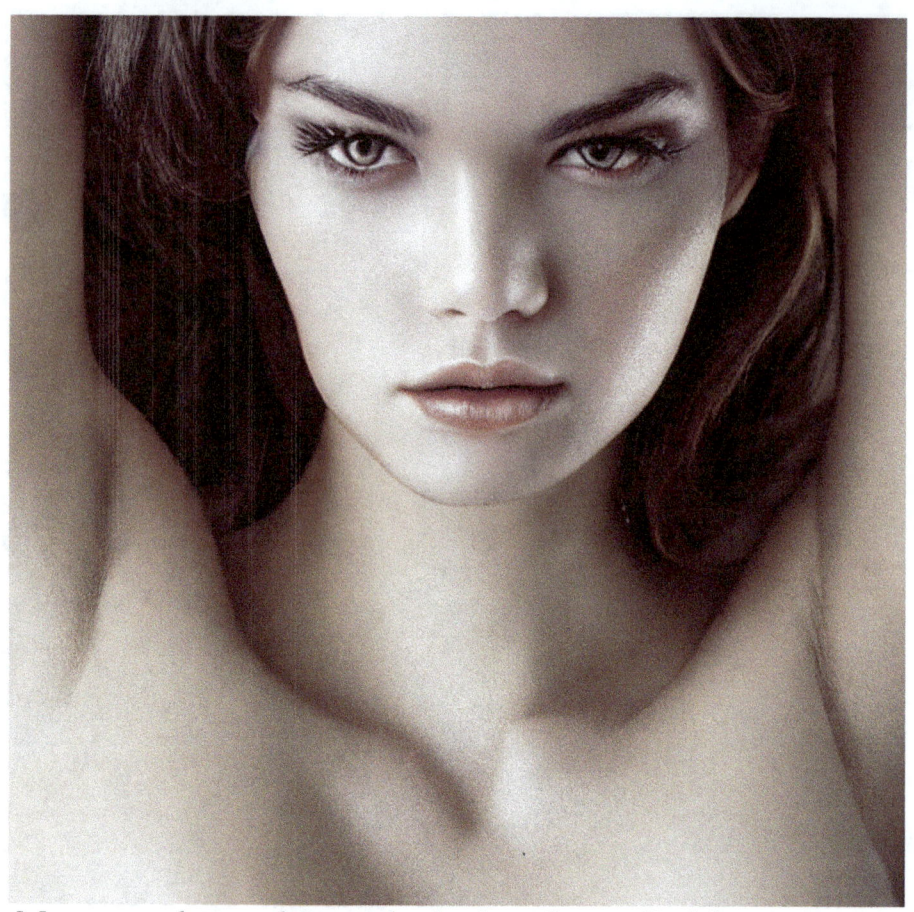

My cover photo - this one had a face fix applied, but it worked really well

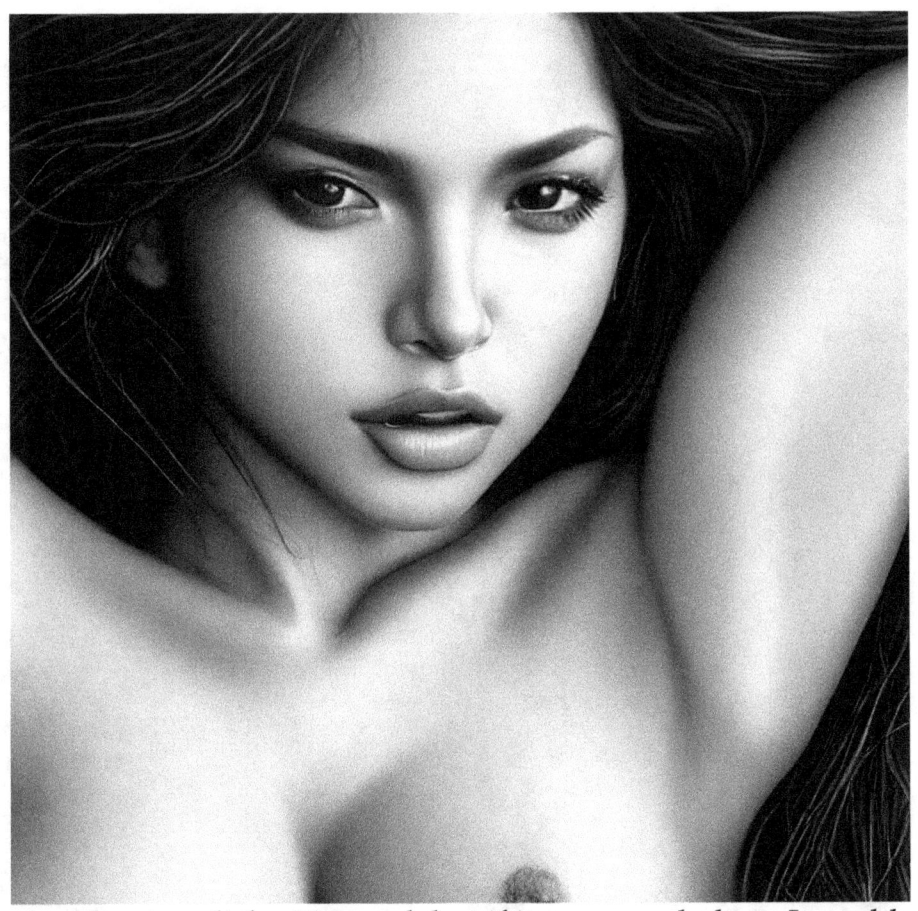

Another too slick - it's good, but if it was a real photo I would say the photographer overworked it

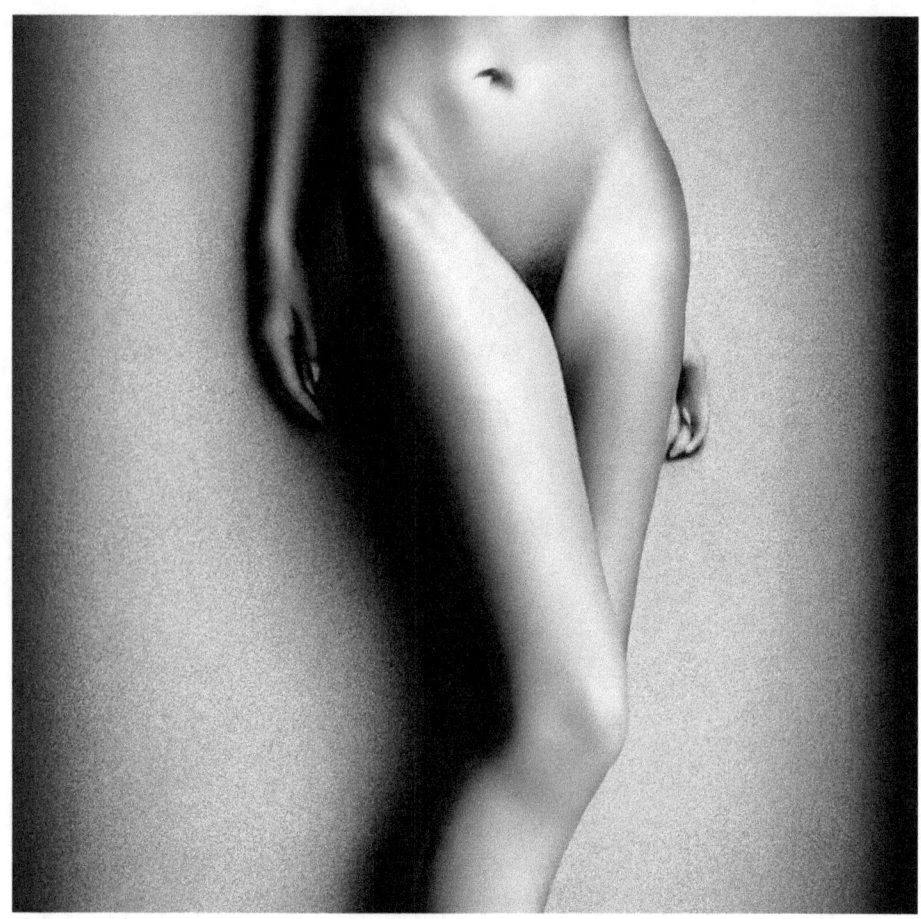
Most of the too slick images are face images, this is an exception

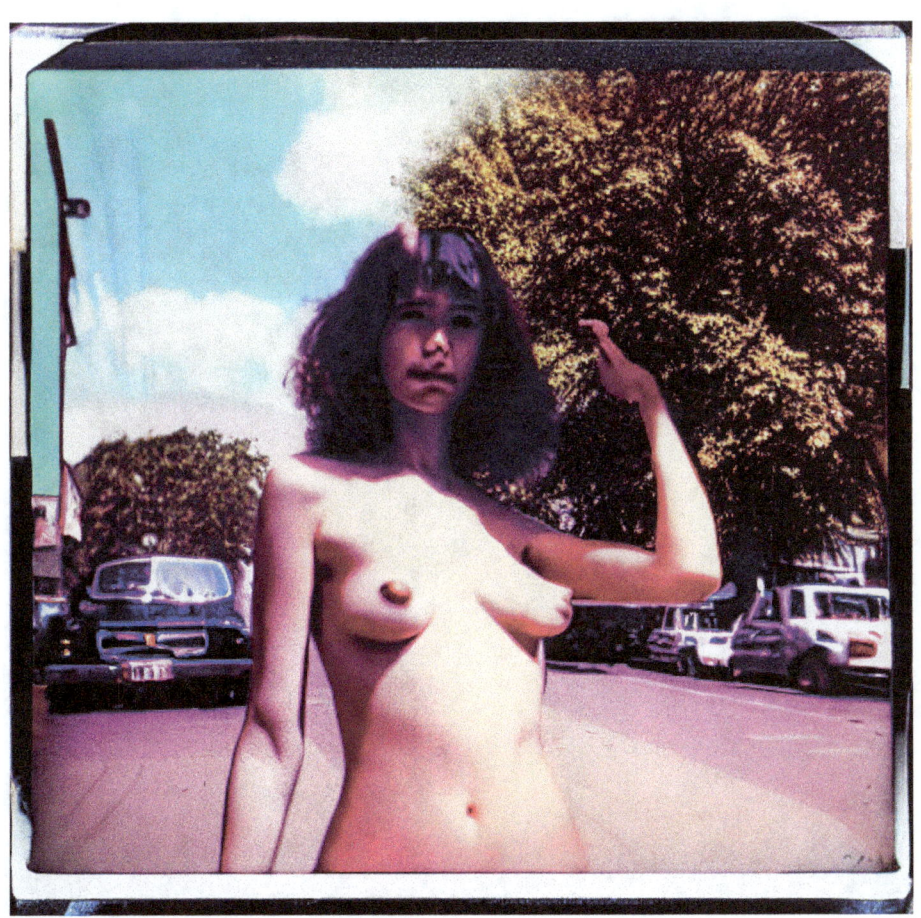
One of the better polaroids

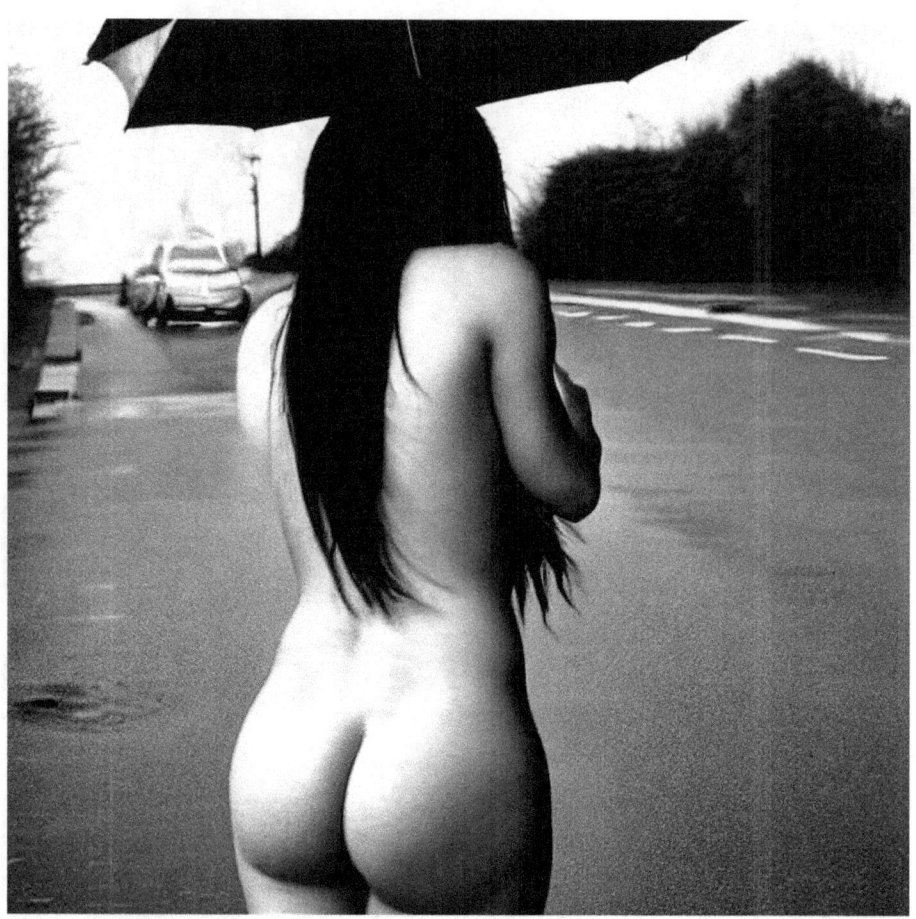

Too artsy for me

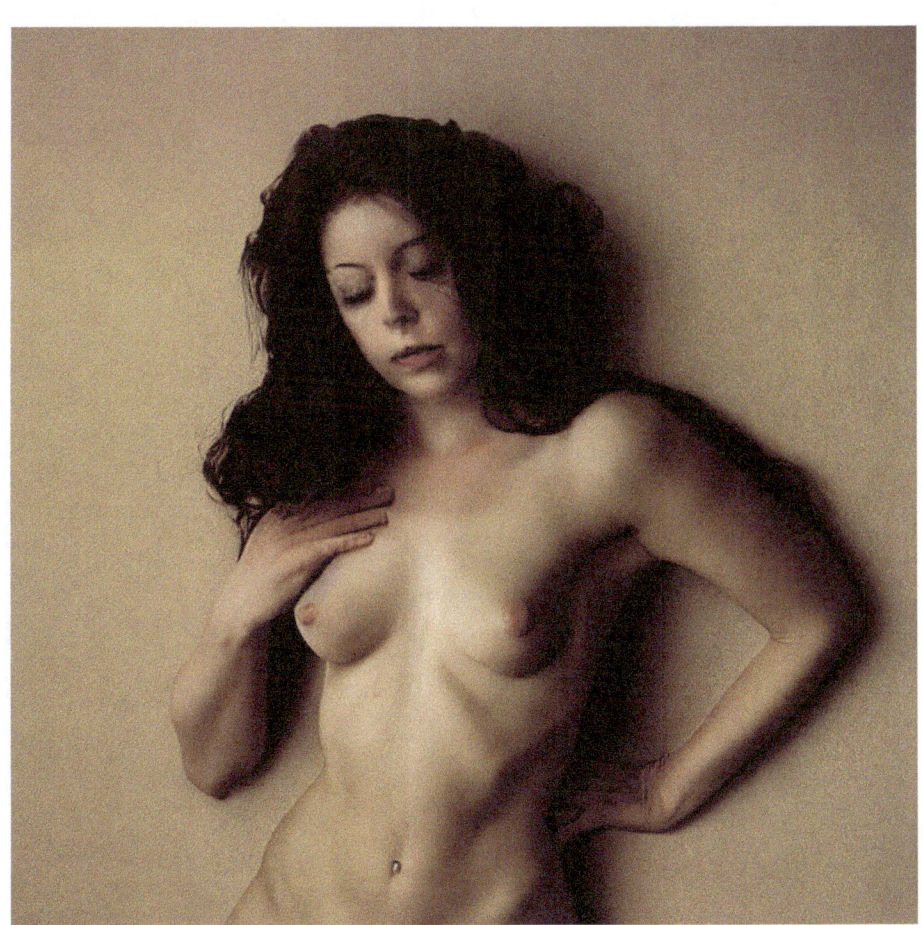

Abs

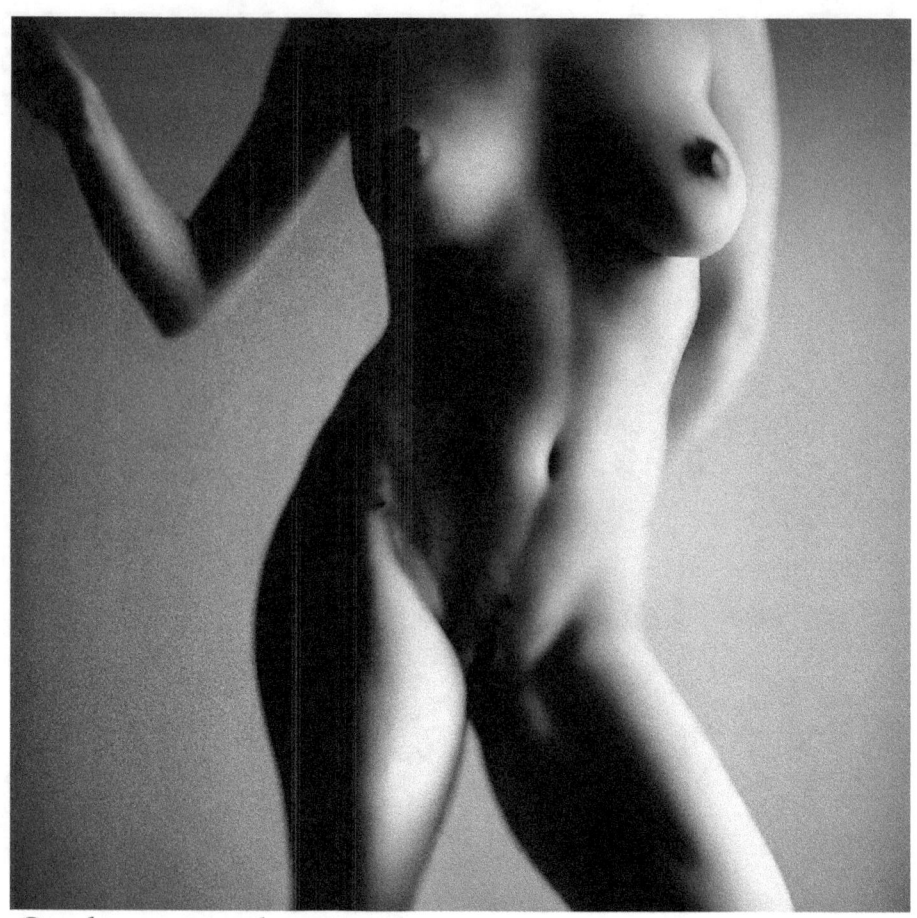
Good tones, good symmetry

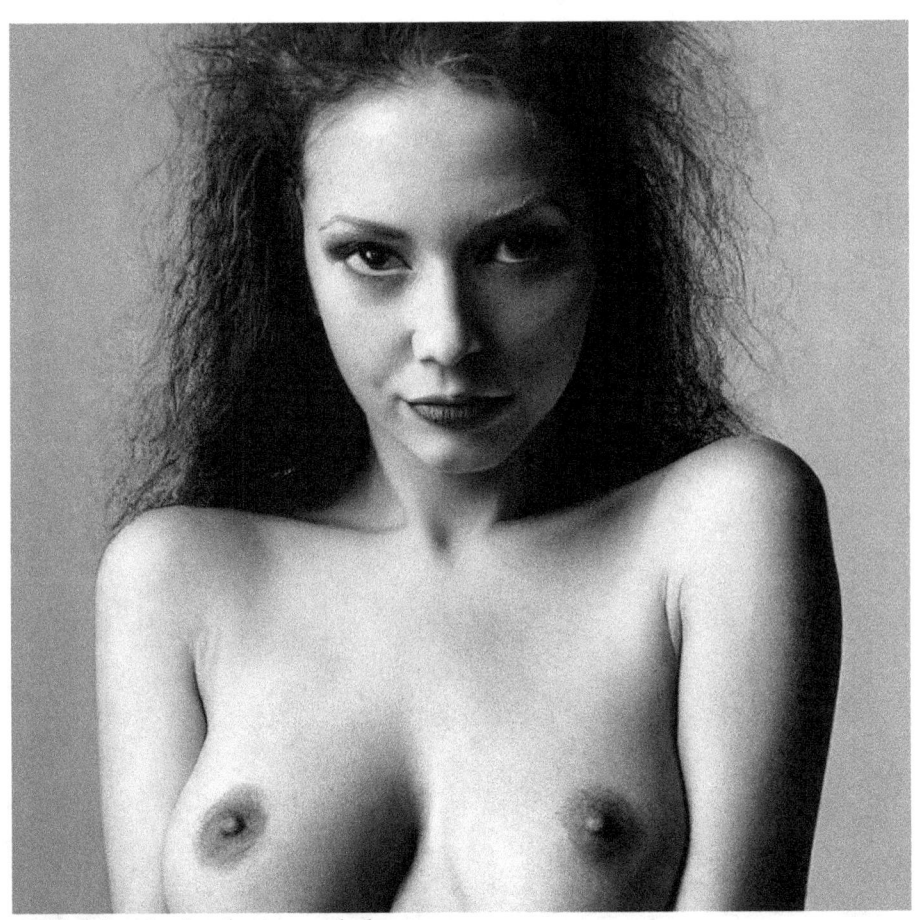
I like both the hair and the eyes

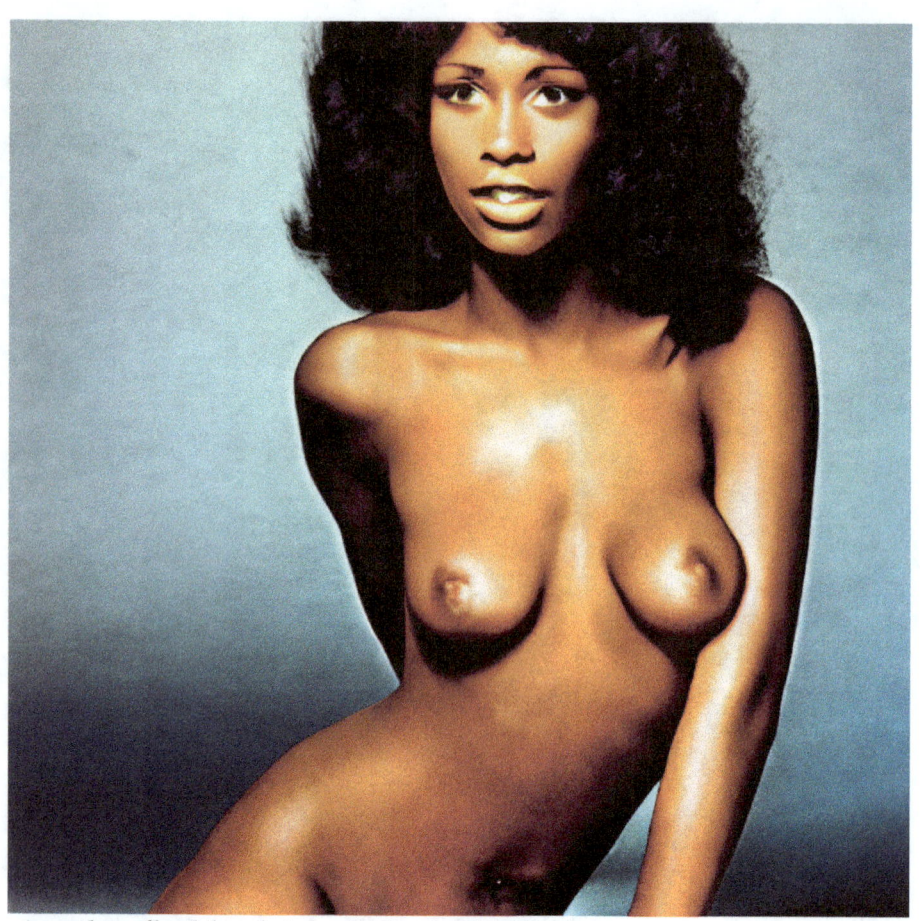
Another flashback image from the 70s

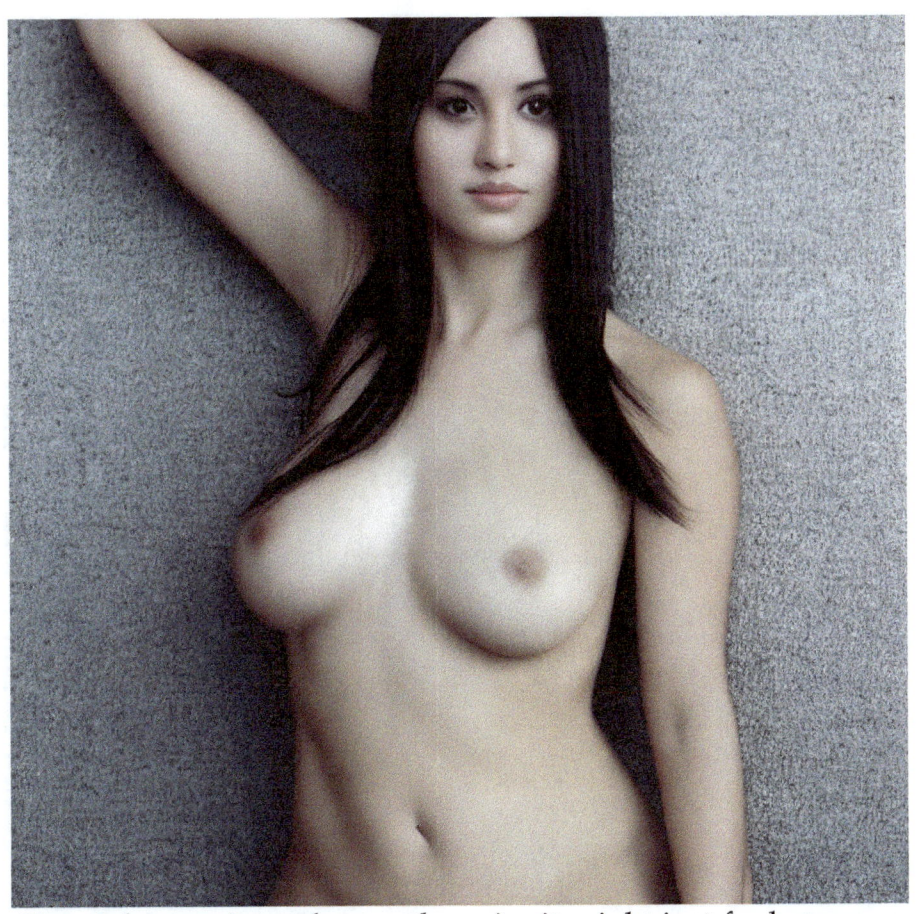
Her right arm is too long, otherwise it might just fool me

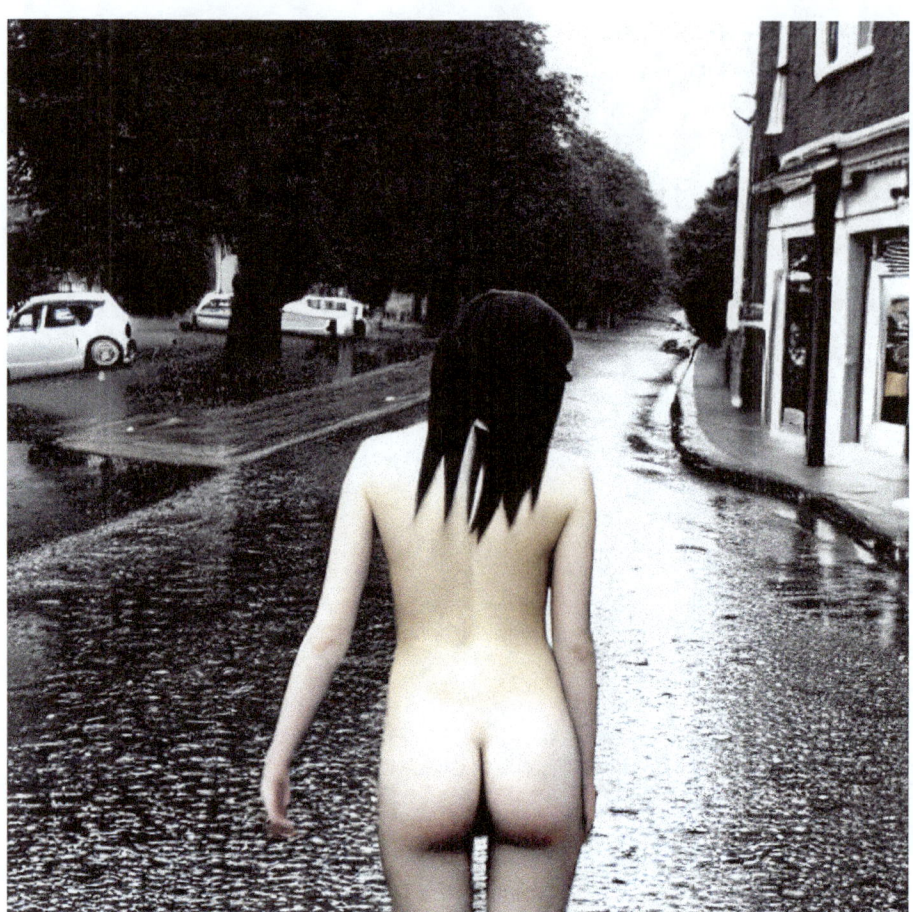
I like the cobbles

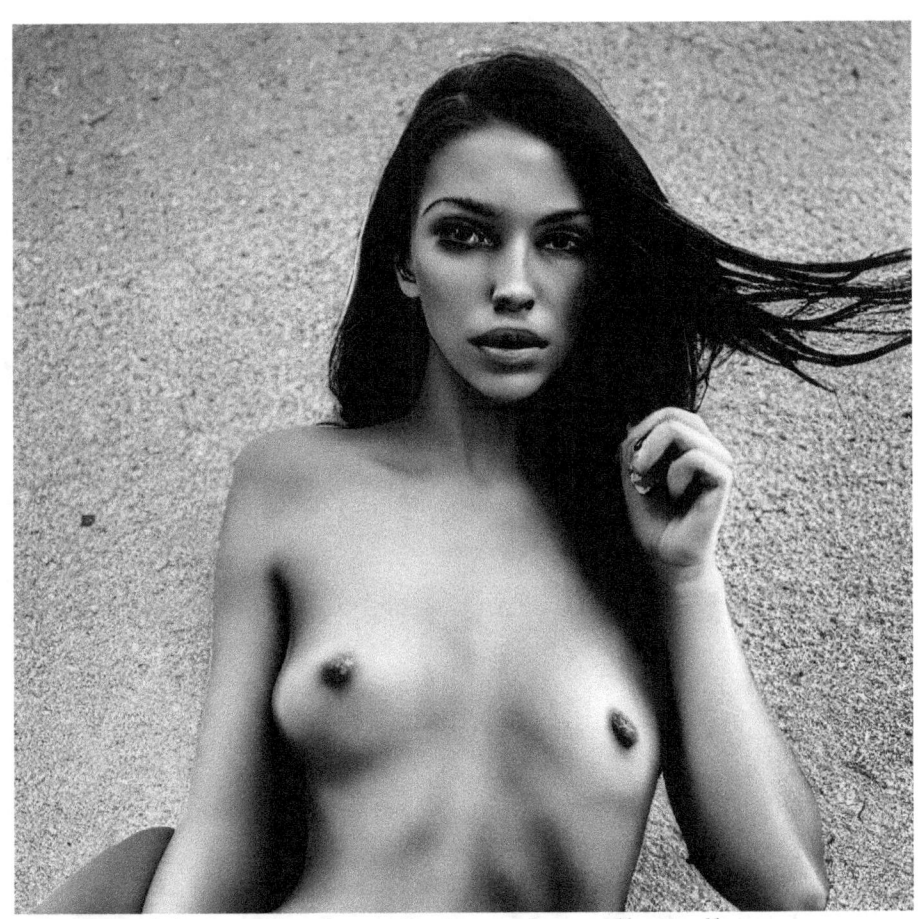
The hand feels off, otherwise it works really well

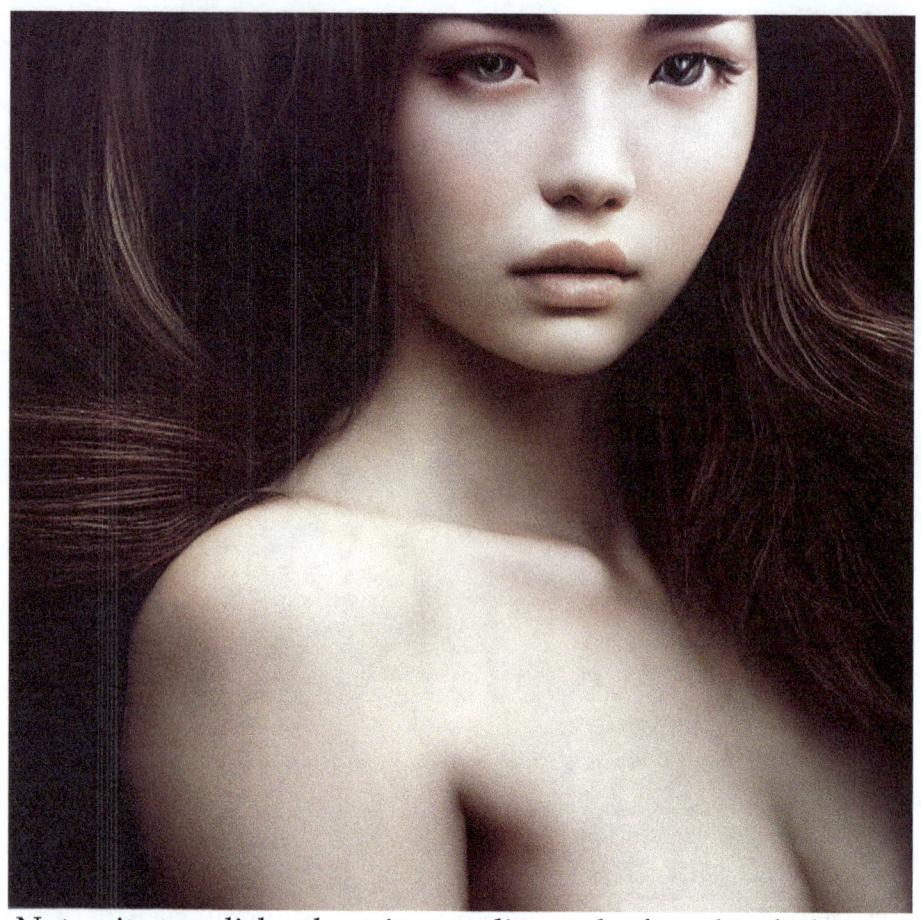

Not quite too slick - there is a quality to the face that feels more real than many of them

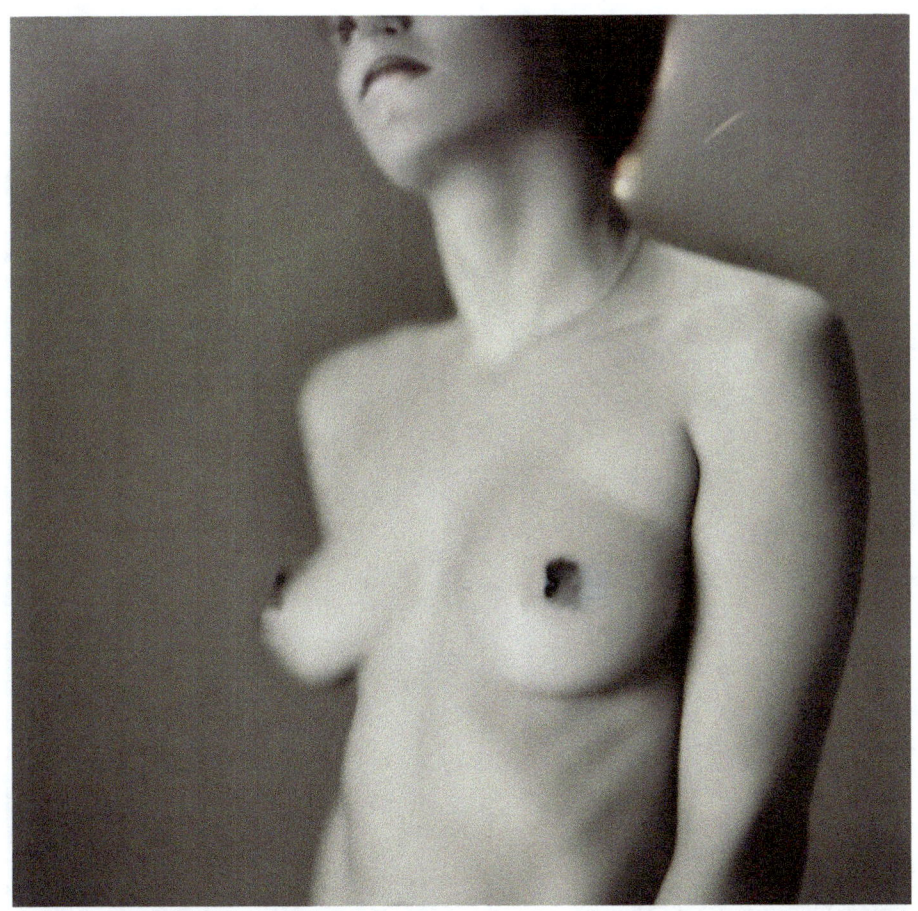

Almost didn't include this one, it's mostly great, but the weird censor thing on the nipples is a bit strange

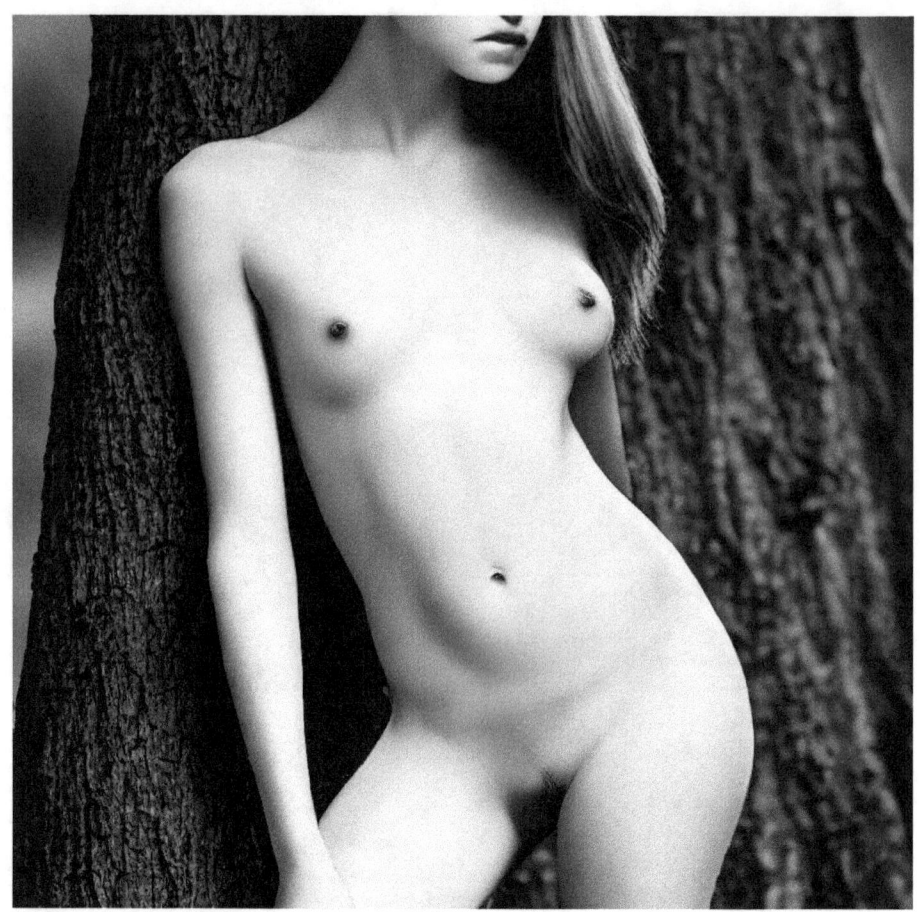
The skin on this one, especially as contrasted to the bark, is what made me include it

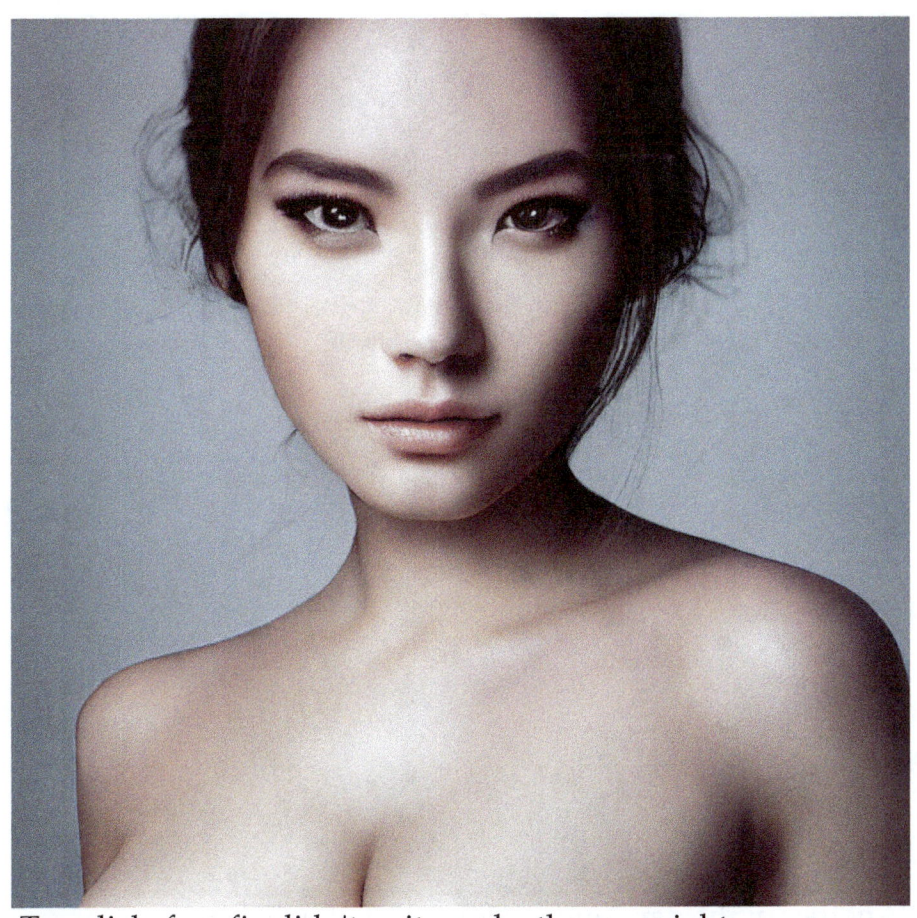

Too slick, face fix didn't quite make the eyes right

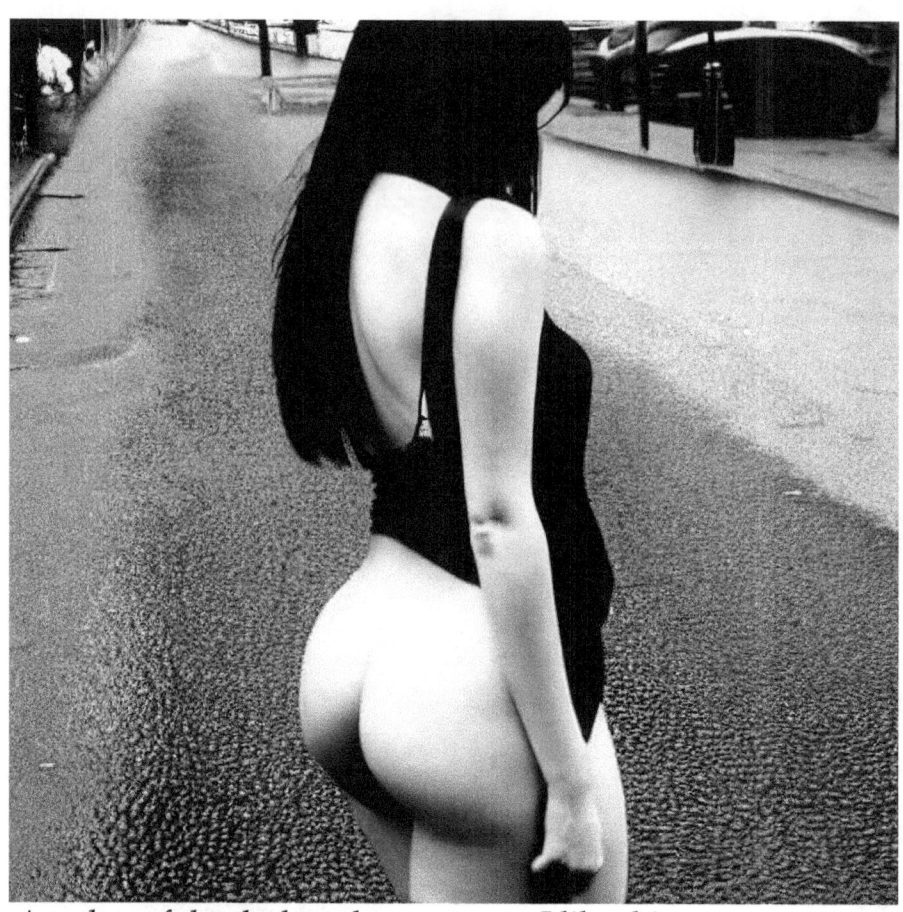

Another of the dark and creepy set - I like this one

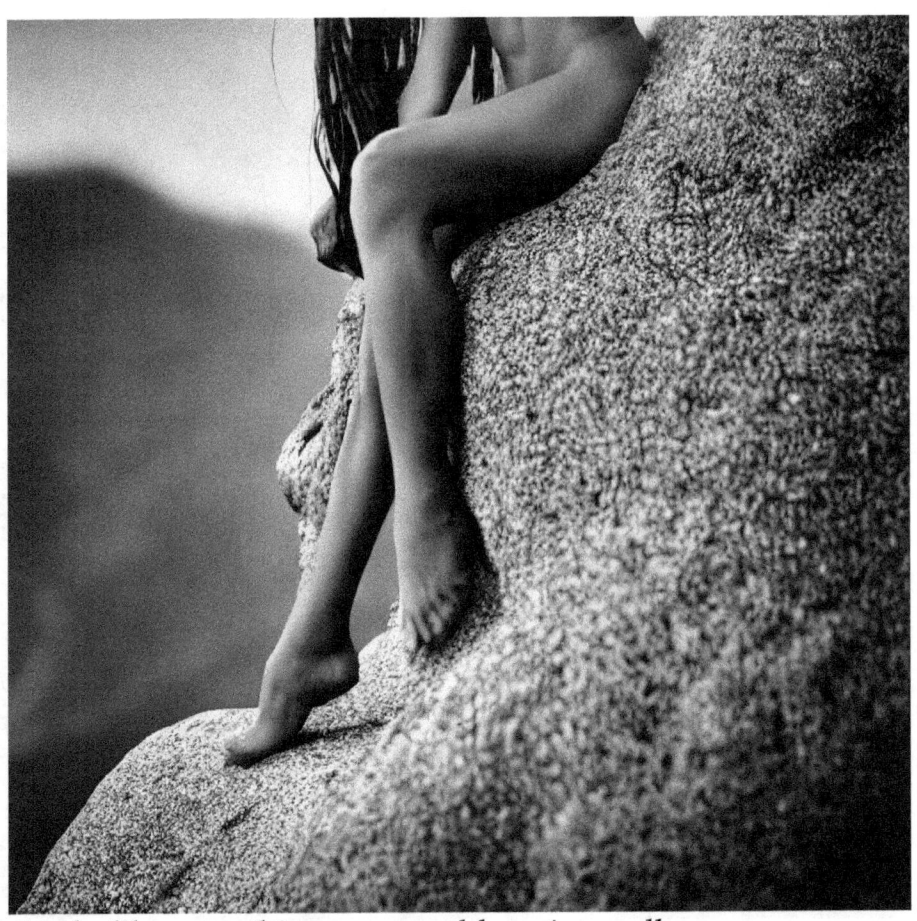
Looks like something you would see in a gallery

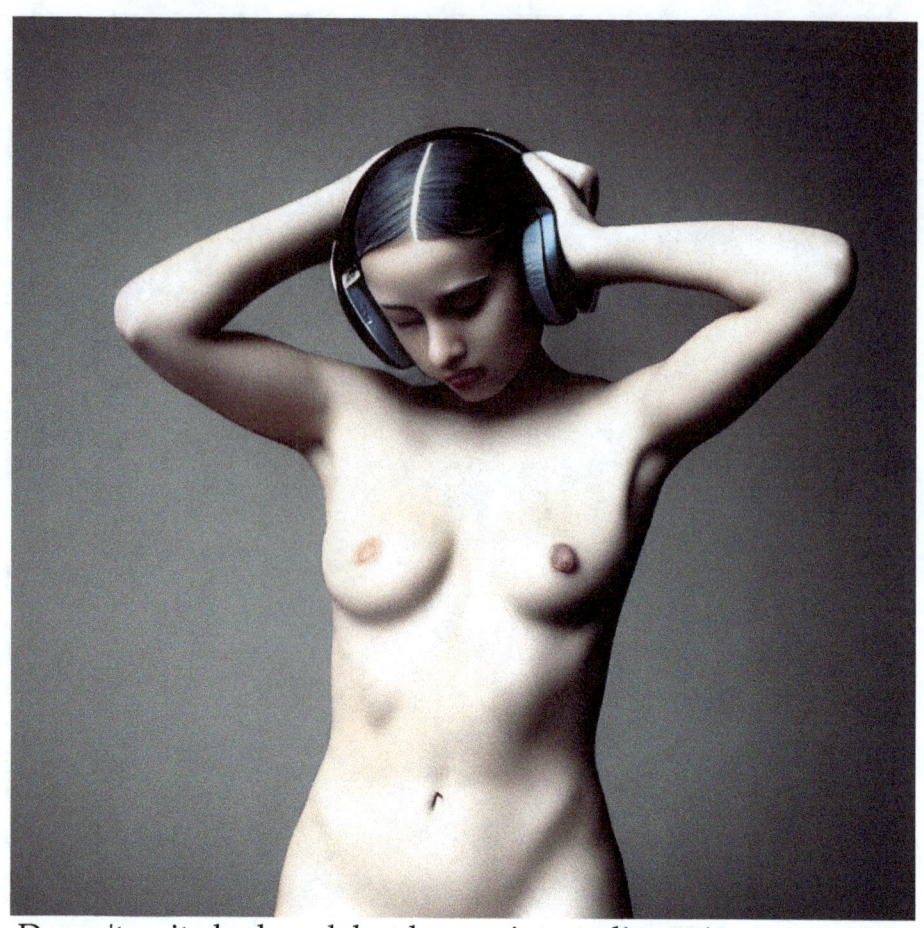
Doesn't quite look real, but has a nice quality to it

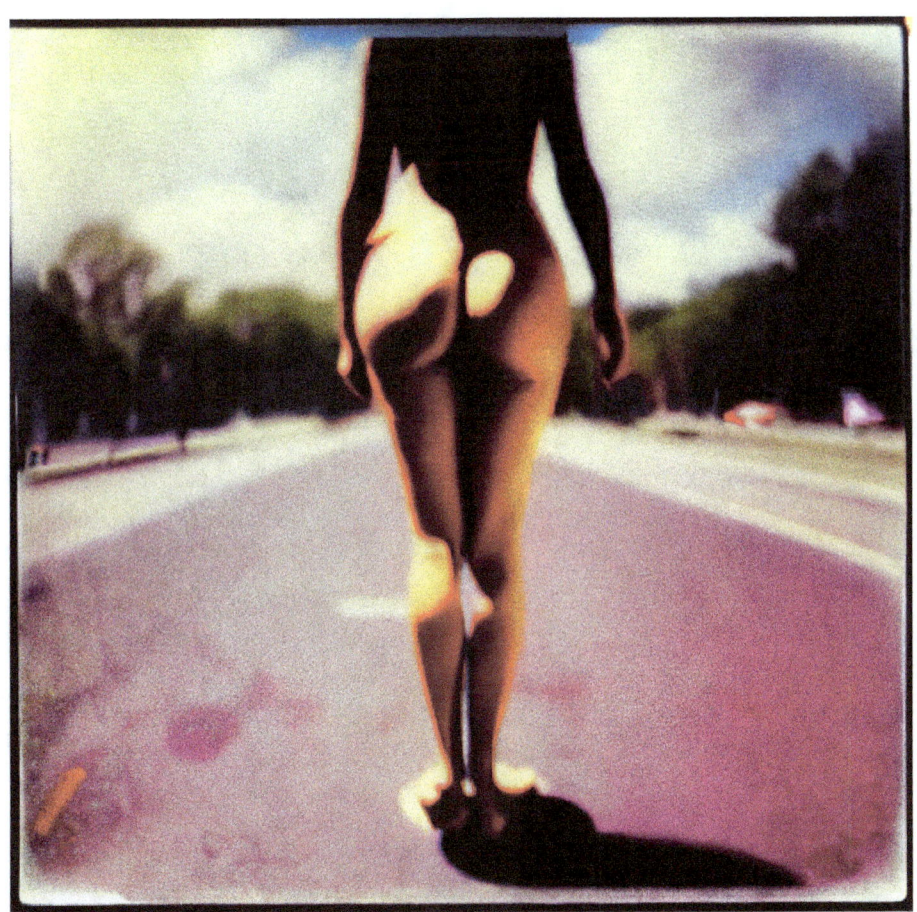
The last of the polaroids

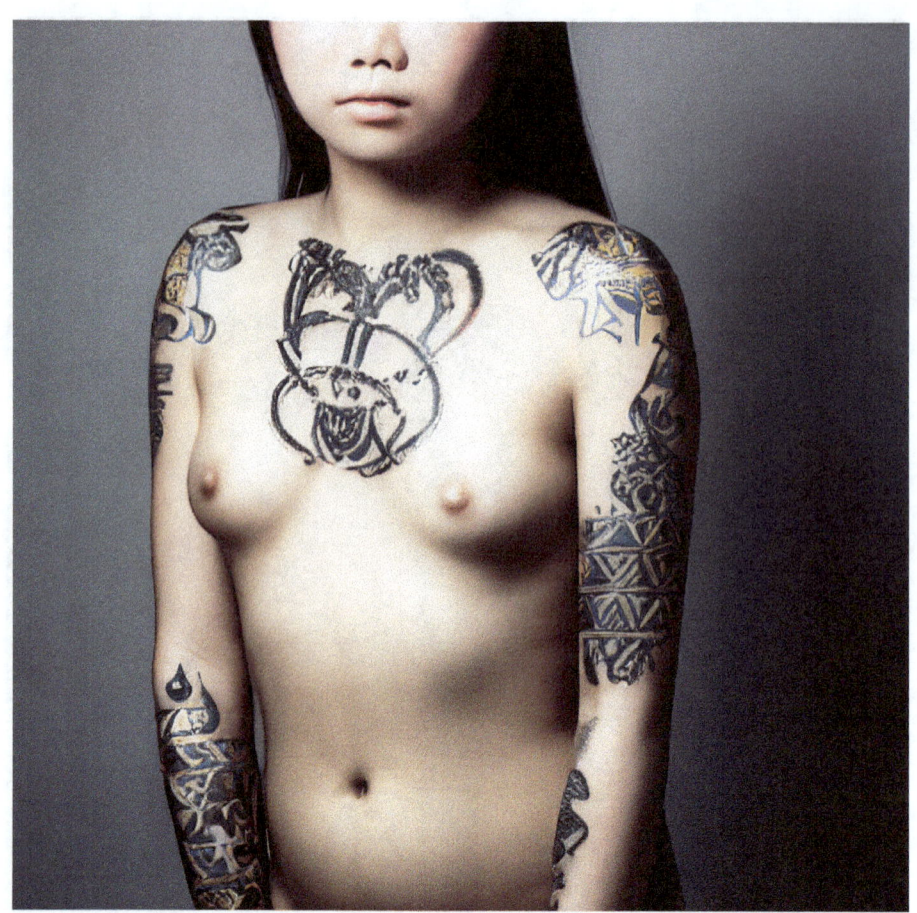
The image that made me believe that this project could actually work. It looks real enough to fool me, and is also a pretty decent image

Jansen Tableau is an amalgam of AI content generation techniques and human editorial processes.

www.ingramcontent.com/pod-product-compliance
Lightning Source LLC
Chambersburg PA
CBHW070157230526
45471CB00002B/703